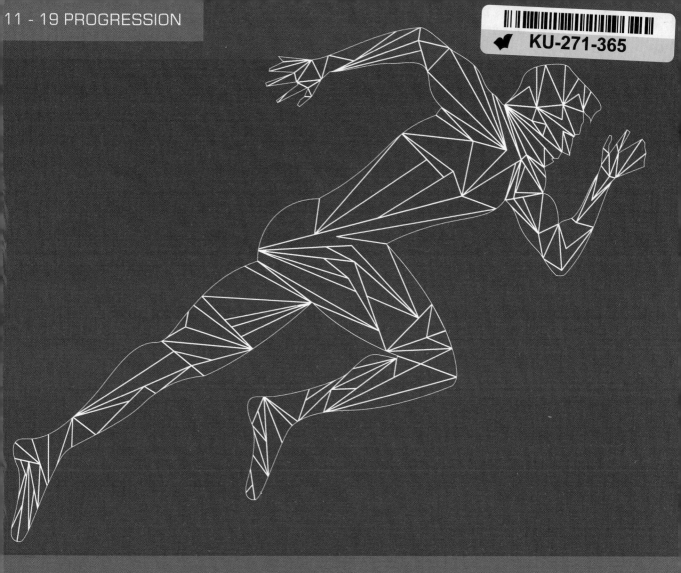

Pearson Edexcel AS and A level Mathematics

Statistics and Mechanics
Year 1/AS

Practice Book

Series Editor: Harry Smith

Authors: Ian Bettison, Laura Connell, Su Nicholson

Pearson

Contents

Contents

How to use this book

The Statistics and Mechanics Year 1/AS Practice Book is designed to be used alongside your Pearson Edexcel AS and A level Mathematics Statistics and Mechanics Year 1/AS textbook. It provides additional practice, including problem-solving and exam-style questions, to help make sure you are ready for your exam.

- The chapters and exercises in this practice book match the chapters and sections in your textbook, so you can easily locate additional practice for any section in the textbook.
- Each chapter finishes with two sets of problem-solving practice questions at three different difficulty levels.
- An Exam question bank at the end of the book provides mixed exam-style questions to help you practise selecting the correct mathematical skills and techniques.

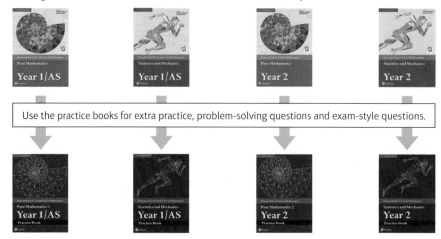

Use the practice books for extra practice, problem-solving questions and exam-style questions.

Finding your way around the book

One-to-one match between exercises in this practice book and sections in your textbook.

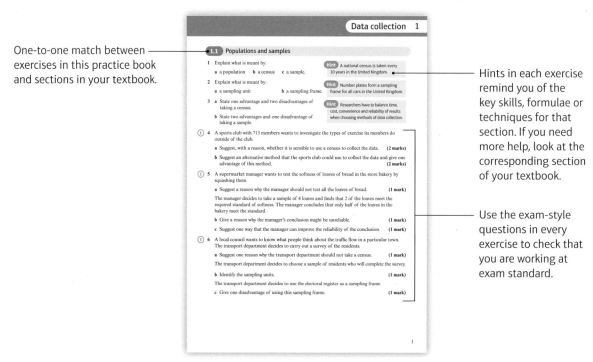

Hints in each exercise remind you of the key skills, formulae or techniques for that section. If you need more help, look at the corresponding section of your textbook.

Use the exam-style questions in every exercise to check that you are working at exam standard.

Exam-style questions are flagged with Ⓔ and have marks allocated to them.

Problem-solving questions are flagged with Ⓟ

Bronze questions might have more steps to lead you through the technique, or require a more straightforward application of the skills from that chapter.

Silver questions are more challenging, and provide less scaffolding. If you're struggling with the Silver question, try the Bronze question first.

You can find more exam-style questions on this chapter in the Exam question bank.

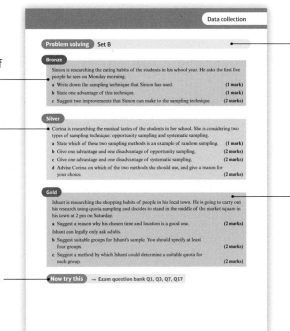

Each chapter ends with two sets of exam-style problem-solving questions which draw on material from throughout the chapter and from earlier chapters.

Gold questions involve tricky problem-solving elements, or might require you to think more creatively. If you can answer the Gold questions then you can be confident that you are ready to tackle the hardest exam questions.

One challenge of the exam is that you aren't usually told which techniques or strategies you need to apply to a particular question. The questions in the Exam question bank are not ordered by topic, so you need to choose the appropriate mathematical skills.

There are a lot more questions in the Exam question bank than there will be on your exam paper. Don't try and tackle them all at once, but make sure you try some of the trickier questions from the end of each section in the question bank.

Published by Pearson Education Limited, 80 Strand, London, WC2R 0RL.

www.pearsonschoolsandfecolleges.co.uk

Text © Pearson Education Limited 2019
Series editor Harry Smith
Edited by Haremi Ltd
Typeset by York Publishing Solutions Pvt. Ltd., INDIA
Original illustrations © Pearson Education Limited 2019
Cover illustration by Marcus, KJA Artists

The rights of Ian Bettison, Laura Connell and Su Nicholson to be identified as authors of this work have been asserted by them in accordance with the Copyright, Designs and Patents Act 1988.

First published 2019

22 21 20 19
10 9 8 7 6 5 4 3 2 1

British Library Cataloguing in Publication Data
A catalogue record for this book is available from the British Library

ISBN 9781292274669

Printed in Italy by L.E.G.O S.p.A

Contains public sector information licensed under the Open Government Licence v3.0.

Note from the publisher
Pearson has robust editorial processes, including answer and fact checks, to ensure the accuracy of the content in this publication, and every effort is made to ensure this publication is free of errors. We are, however, only human, and occasionally errors do occur. Pearson is not liable for any misunderstandings that arise as a result of errors in this publication, but it is our priority to ensure that the content is accurate. If you spot an error, please do contact us at resourcescorrections@pearson.com so we can make sure it is corrected.

1.1 Populations and samples

1 Explain what is meant by:

    a a population   **b** a census   **c** a sample.

> **Hint** A national census is taken every 10 years in the United Kingdom.

2 Explain what is meant by:

    a a sampling unit   **b** a sampling frame.

> **Hint** Number plates form a sampling frame for all cars in the United Kingdom.

3 **a** State one advantage and two disadvantages of taking a census.

    b State two advantages and one disadvantage of taking a sample.

> **Hint** Researchers have to balance time, cost, convenience and reliability of results when choosing methods of data collection.

4 A sports club with 713 members wants to investigate the types of exercise its members do outside of the club.

    a Suggest, with a reason, whether it is sensible to use a census to collect the data.   **(2 marks)**

    b Suggest an alternative method that the sports club could use to collect the data and give one advantage of this method.   **(2 marks)**

5 A supermarket manager wants to test the softness of loaves of bread in the store bakery by squashing them.

    a Suggest a reason why the manager should not test all the loaves of bread.   **(1 mark)**

The manager decides to take a sample of 4 loaves and finds that 2 of the loaves meet the required standard of softness. The manager concludes that only half of the loaves in the bakery meet the standard.

    b Give a reason why the manager's conclusion might be unreliable.   **(1 mark)**

    c Suggest one way that the manager can improve the reliability of the conclusion.   **(1 mark)**

6 A local council wants to know what people think about the traffic flow in a particular town. The transport department decides to carry out a survey of the residents.

    a Suggest one reason why the transport department should not take a census.   **(1 mark)**

The transport department decides to choose a sample of residents who will complete the survey.

    b Identify the sampling units.   **(1 mark)**

The transport department decides to use the electoral register as a sampling frame.

    c Give one disadvantage of using this sampling frame.   **(1 mark)**

E/P **7** A manufacturer of light bulbs is testing the lifetime of the bulbs. The manufacturer switches the bulbs on and records the number of hours each bulb is lit before it blows.

    a Explain why the manufacturer should take a sample rather than a census. **(1 mark)**

    The manufacturer tests a sample of three bulbs and obtains the following results:

        762 hours   851 hours   801 hours

    b The company claims that the lifetime of its bulbs is 800 hours.

        i Use the sample data to comment on this claim.

        ii Suggest one way in which the manufacturer can improve its prediction about the lifetime of a bulb. **(3 marks)**

1.2 Sampling

1   **a** Explain what is meant by a simple random sample.

    b Explain how you would take a simple random sample of size 20 from a population of 100.

> **Hint** You can use your calculator to generate random numbers.

2   **a** Explain what is meant by a systematic sample.

    b Explain how you would take a systematic sample of size 20 from a population of 100.

> **Hint** Work out the proportion of the population that you are going to sample.

3   **a** Explain what is meant by a stratified sample.

    b Explain how you would take a stratified sample of size 20 from a population composed of 40 males and 60 females.

> **Hint** Work out the proportion of males and females in the population.

E/P **4** A dance school teacher wants to take a sample of the school's members. Each member has a unique ID number.

    a State two advantages of using simple random sampling. **(2 marks)**

    There are 75 boys and 125 girls at the school.

    b Using this information, state one disadvantage of using simple random sampling. **(1 mark)**

    The teacher decides to use a stratified sampling method.

    c Explain how the teacher can take a stratified sample of size 40. **(2 marks)**

E/P **5** A company wants to take a sample of its employees. There are 700 employees and each has a unique employee number.

    a Explain how the company could take a systematic sample of size 35 from the employees. **(2 marks)**

    It is known that the management team all have employee numbers ending in 0.

    b Using this information, state one disadvantage of using a systematic sample. **(2 marks)**

P **6** A school wants to carry out an investigation into the eating habits of its students. There are 1200 students in the school.

    a Explain how the school could take a simple random sample of size 50 from the students and state one disadvantage of using this sampling method. **(2 marks)**

    b Suggest a better sampling method and explain how the school should take this sample.

                                                  (3 marks)

1.3 Non-random sampling

1 **a** Explain what is meant by opportunity sampling.

Researchers want to investigate the habits of shoppers in a town's high street.

    b Explain how they might select an opportunity sample of size 20.

> **Hint** Opportunity sampling and quota sampling are examples of non-random sampling methods. Using non-random sampling methods can introduce bias.

2 **a** Explain what is meant by quota sampling.

Researchers want to investigate people's attitudes to advertising in the cinema.

    b Explain how they might select a quota sample of size 30.

> **Hint** Make sure your answer refers to the context of the question.

P **3** A coach of a basketball team wants to take a sample from all the players on the team. The coach has a list of the players in order of height.

    a Explain how the coach can carry out an opportunity sample of size 5. **(1 mark)**

    b State one disadvantage of using an opportunity sample in this context. **(1 mark)**

    c Suggest an alternative sampling method that could be used and explain how the coach can take this sample. **(2 marks)**

P **4** Researchers are collecting data on the number of hours of television watched by people in a local village. They ask the first four people they see coming out of the cinema on a Tuesday evening.

    a Describe the sampling method used and comment on the reliability of the data gathered.

                                                  (2 marks)

    b Suggest two ways to improve the method used by the researchers. **(2 marks)**

P **5** A researcher wants to investigate the types of car owned by people living on a housing estate. It is known that there are 150 male drivers and 200 female drivers on the particular estate.

    a Explain how the researcher can take a quota sample of size 70. **(2 marks)**

    b State one key difference between quota sampling and stratified sampling. **(1 mark)**

    c Give one advantage of using quota sampling over stratified sampling. **(1 mark)**

The researcher stands at the entrance to the estate. For each car entering the estate, the researcher notes the gender of the driver and the type of car.

    d Criticise this method of collecting the data. **(2 marks)**

1.4 Types of data

1 State whether the following variables are qualitative or quantitative:

a height of a house **b** hair colour

c time taken to run 50 m.

> **Hint** **Quantitative** data can be recorded as a numerical observation. **Qualitative** data must be recorded as words or categories.

2 State whether the following variables are discrete or continuous:

a length of a worm **b** number of slugs

c height of an ant.

> **Hint** Variables that can take any value in a given range are **continuous**. Variables that can only take specific values are **discrete**.

(E) 3 The table shows the masses of children on a summer camp.

Mass, x (kg)	Frequency
$35 \leqslant x < 40$	14
$40 \leqslant x < 45$	18
$45 \leqslant x < 50$	12
$50 \leqslant x < 55$	7

a Explain why the data in the table is continuous. **(1 mark)**

b For the third group, write down:

  i the class boundaries **ii** the class width **iii** the midpoint. **(3 marks)**

(E/P) 4 The table shows the numbers of caterpillars found on each tree in a forest.

Number of caterpillars	Number of trees
7	78
8	45
9	63
10	18

a State whether this data is discrete or continuous. **(1 mark)**

A researcher wants to see if there is a relationship between the number of caterpillars on each tree and the lengths of the caterpillars.

b Explain how the researcher can take a stratified sample of size 20 from all of the trees in the forest. **(2 marks)**

The researcher measures the lengths of the caterpillars on each of the sampled trees.

c Describe the type of data the researcher is collecting. **(1 mark)**

1.5 The large data set

1 From the five UK weather stations featured in the large data set, write down the station that is furthest:

   a north   b south   c west.

Hint You need to know the approximate locations of all the weather stations in the large data set.

2 Explain what is meant by:

   a daily total rainfall   b daily maximum gust.

Hint You need to know the units for all of the data set variables.

P 3 Delilah is interested in how the daily total sunshine changes the further north you go. She chooses five days, at random, from the large data set for Heathrow and Hurn in 2015.

   a Criticise:

   i her sample size   ii her choices of location.   **(2 marks)**

   b Explain how Delilah can take a simple random sample of size 15 from the large data set for Heathrow in 2015.   **(2 marks)**

   During her sampling, Delilah selects the same date twice.

   c Explain why this is wrong and describe how she could correctly generate her sample.

        (2 marks)

P 4 From the large data set, Jerome calculates the average mean daily temperature for Leuchars and Camborne in 2015 using a random sample of 5 days from each location.

   a Give a geographical reason why the average mean daily temperature for Leuchars might be lower than for Camborne.   **(1 mark)**

   b Criticise Jerome's sampling method and suggest an improvement.   **(2 marks)**

P 5 Amara is investigating daily total rainfall in Leeming in 2015.

   a Explain how she can take a systematic sample of size 20 from the data.   **(2 marks)**

   She finds that on several days, the reading is recorded as 'tr'.
   She discards these readings and chooses additional readings for her sample.

   b State the meaning of 'tr', and evaluate Amara's method.   **(2 marks)**

   c Suggest how Amara should deal with 'tr' readings in her investigation.   **(1 mark)**

P 6 Jagdeep records the daily mean windspeed for a randomly chosen day in June 1987 in Hurn as 31 knots. He records the daily maximum gust on the same day as 25 knots.

   a Explain why Jagdeep must have recorded at least one of the values incorrectly.   **(1 mark)**

   The correct value for the daily mean windspeed is in fact 11 knots.

   b Convert this reading using the Beaufort scale, giving your answer as both a number and a description.   **(2 marks)**

E/P **7** A researcher is investigating average weather conditions in July 2015 in Beijing, Perth and Hurn. The researcher records the following data:

Location	A	B	C
Average temperature (°C)	16.8	26.8	13.3
Average windspeed (kn)	8.3	4.0	7.4

© Crown Copyright Met Office

Using your knowledge of the large data set, suggest the name of the weather station that is recorded as:

a location A   **b** location B   **c** location C.   **(3 marks)**

Problem solving   Set A

Bronze

Joanna is investigating the daily total rainfall in Perth in 2015.
She uses the large data set to select a sample from all 184 days.

a Describe how Joanna could take a random sample of 5 days.   **(2 marks)**

b Give one advantage and one disadvantage of using a random sample.   **(2 marks)**

c Suggest one improvement that Joanna can make to improve the reliability of the data she collects.   **(2 marks)**

Silver

Francine is investigating the daily mean windspeed for Beijing for August, September and October 2015. She uses the large data set to select a sample of size 20 by generating a random starting number between 1 and 5 and choosing every fifth value thereafter.

a Describe the sampling method that Francine has used.   **(1 mark)**

b Using your knowledge of the large data set, explain why Francine's method will not generate a sample of size 20.   **(2 marks)**

Gold

Ali is investigating the daily mean wind direction in May, June and July in Jacksonville in 2015. He uses the large data set to select a sample from all 92 days.

a Describe how Ali can select a sample of size 15 stratified by month.   **(2 marks)**

b Give one advantage of using a stratified sample in this context.   **(1 mark)**

c Describe the two ways that Ali's data is recorded in the large data set.   **(2 marks)**

Problem solving   Set B

Bronze

Simon is researching the eating habits of the students in his school year. He asks the first five people he sees on Monday morning.

a   Write down the sampling technique that Simon has used.   **(1 mark)**

b   State one advantage of this technique.   **(1 mark)**

c   Suggest two improvements that Simon can make to the sampling technique.   **(2 marks)**

Silver

Corina is researching the musical tastes of the students in her school. She is considering two types of sampling technique: opportunity sampling and systematic sampling.

a   State which of these two sampling methods is an example of random sampling.   **(1 mark)**

b   Give one advantage and one disadvantage of opportunity sampling.   **(2 marks)**

c   Give one advantage and one disadvantage of systematic sampling.   **(2 marks)**

d   Advise Corina on which of the two methods she should use, and give a reason for your choice.   **(2 marks)**

Gold

Ishant is researching the shopping habits of people in his local town. He is going to carry out his research using quota sampling and decides to stand in the middle of the market square in his town at 2 pm on Saturday.

a   Suggest a reason why his chosen time and location is a good one.   **(2 marks)**

Ishant can legally only ask adults.

b   Suggest suitable groups for Ishant's sample. You should specify at least four groups.   **(2 marks)**

c   Suggest a method by which Ishant could determine a suitable quota for each group.   **(2 marks)**

Now try this   → **Exam question bank Q1, Q3, Q7, Q17**

2 Measures of location and spread

2.1 Measures of central tendency

1 The masses, in grams, of 9 pieces of cheese are:

   550 450 300 400 450 500 450 300 600

   Calculate:

   a the mode   **b** the mean   **c** the median.

   > **Hint** To find the median, put the data in ascending order.

2 The table shows the frequency distribution for the numbers of eggs in the nests of a group of blackbirds.

Number of eggs	2	3	4	5	6
Frequency	6	11	13	7	2

   Find:

   a the mode   **b** the mean   **c** the median.

   > **Hint** To calculate the mean, use the formula $\bar{x} = \dfrac{\sum xf}{\sum f}$

3 The table shows the times taken by a group of students to walk to school.

Time, t (mins)	$10 \leqslant t < 15$	$15 \leqslant t < 20$	$20 \leqslant t < 25$	$25 \leqslant t < 30$
Frequency	5	14	7	2

   a Write down the modal class.

   b Calculate an estimate for the mean time taken to walk to school.

   > **Hint** Use the midpoint of each class interval.

(E/P) 4 In class 12B, there are 13 girls and 11 boys. The mean height of the girls is 1.60 m and the mean height of the boys is 1.71 m. Calculate the mean height of all 24 pupils.   **(3 marks)**

(E) 5 Bill is shelling peas. He records the number of peas inside each pod and uses a frequency table to show his results.

Number of peas	4	5	6	7	8
Frequency	12	15	18	11	7

   a Write down the median for this data.   **(1 mark)**

   b Calculate the mean number of peas per pod.   **(1 mark)**

   He opens one more pod and discovers it contains 7 peas.

   c Write down the effect that including this piece of data will have on the mean.   **(1 mark)**

6 A convenience store manager records the amounts of time customers spend in the store.

Time, t (mins)	$2 \leqslant t < 4$	$4 \leqslant t < 6$	$6 \leqslant t < 8$	$8 \leqslant t < 10$
Frequency	7	9	12	6

  a Write down the modal class. **(1 mark)**

  b Calculate an estimate for the mean amount of time spent in the store. **(1 mark)**

  c Explain why your answer to part **b** is an estimate. **(1 mark)**

7 Using data compiled from the large data set, the table shows the mean daily temperatures in Jacksonville during May 2015.

Temp, t (°C)	$16 \leqslant t < 18$	$18 \leqslant t < 20$	$20 \leqslant t < 22$	$22 \leqslant t < 24$	$24 \leqslant t < 26$	$26 \leqslant t < 28$
Frequency	1	3	2	9	13	3

© Crown Copyright Met Office

  a Write down the modal class. **(1 mark)**

  b Calculate an estimate for the mean daily temperature. **(1 mark)**

2.2 Other measures of location

1 The masses, in grams, of seven gold ingots are:

  324 313 315 372 377 312 369

Write down:

  a the lower quartile   **b** the upper quartile.

Hint Put the data in ascending order first.

2 The table shows the frequency distribution of the numbers of siblings in a group of families.

Number of siblings	1	2	3	4	5
Frequency	7	12	15	11	6

Write down:

  a the median   **b** the upper quartile

  c the lower quartile.

Hint Find half of n, a quarter of n and three quarters of n. If these are not whole numbers, round up and pick this data point.

3 The table shows the distances travelled by a group of students to get to school.

Distance, x (km)	$1 \leqslant x < 3$	$3 \leqslant x < 5$	$5 \leqslant x < 7$	$7 \leqslant x < 9$
Frequency	6	8	5	3

  a Use linear interpolation to estimate the median distance travelled.

  b Use linear interpolation to estimate the upper quartile.

Hint Work out which classes contain the median and upper quartile. Then use proportion to estimate out how far through each class the measure of location will be found.

9

E/P **4** Jonas records the number of books on each of 14 shelves in his library:

    13 14 12 18 20 14 17
    15 15 21 20 15 17 20

  a Calculate the median number of books. **(2 marks)**

  b Calculate the lower quartile. **(2 marks)**

E/P **5** The masses, in kg, of some students are recorded in the table.

Mass, m (kg)	$40 \leqslant m < 45$	$45 \leqslant m < 50$	$50 \leqslant m < 55$	$55 \leqslant m < 60$
Frequency	7	10	14	5

  a Use linear interpolation to find an estimate for the median mass. **(2 marks)**

  b Explain why your answer to part **a** is an estimate. **(1 mark)**

E/P **6** The lengths, in cm, of a group of slowworms are recorded in the table.

Length, x (cm)	$25 \leqslant x < 30$	$30 \leqslant x < 35$	$35 \leqslant x < 40$	$40 \leqslant x$
Frequency	25	28	17	12

  a Use linear interpolation to estimate:

    i the median length

    ii the 70th percentile. **(3 marks)**

  b Explain why it is not possible to estimate the 90th percentile in this way. **(1 mark)**

E/P **7** The lengths of train delays at a station on a particular day are recorded in the table.

Time, t (mins)	$1 \leqslant t < 3$	$3 \leqslant t < 5$	$5 \leqslant t < 10$	$10 \leqslant t < 20$
Frequency	6	13	18	4

  a Estimate the 60th percentile. **(2 marks)**

  b State one assumption you have made in your answer to part **a**. **(1 mark)**

The station advertises that fewer than 20% of trains are delayed by more than 8 minutes.

  c By calculating a suitable percentile, comment on the validity of this claim. **(3 marks)**

2.3 Measures of spread

1 The lengths, in cm, of 9 dachshunds are:

    45 48 52 60 51 53 47 49 50

  a Find the range for this data.

  b Calculate the interquartile range.

Hint Put the data in ascending order first.

Interquartile range = $Q_3 - Q_1$

2 The table shows the number of pets owned by a class of students.

Number of pets	0	1	2	3	4
Frequency	2	6	8	13	1

Calculate:

a the range   **b** the interquartile range.

Hint For part **b**, work out Q_1 and Q_3 first.

3 The table shows the lengths of time, in minutes, it takes 31 students to complete a test.

Time, t (mins)	$40 \leqslant t < 42$	$42 \leqslant t < 44$	$44 \leqslant t < 46$	$46 \leqslant t < 48$
Frequency	2	15	11	3

a Write down an estimate for the range.

b Calculate an estimate for the interquartile range.

Hint For part **b**, use linear interpolation to find Q_1 and Q_3.

P 4 From the large data set, the daily mean windspeeds (knots) in Beijing for the first 10 days of May 2015 are:

    5.5   3.8   7.5   8.0   5.5   4.0   5.3   5.0   3.3   3.5

a Calculate the median and interquartile range.   **(2 marks)**

The median daily mean windspeed in Beijing for the first 10 days of June 2015 was 4.1 knots and the interquartile range was 3 knots.

b Compare the data for May with the data for June.   **(2 marks)**

P 5 The masses, in grams, of a group of 4-week-old kittens are recorded in the table.

Mass, m (g)	$400 \leqslant m < 425$	$425 \leqslant m < 450$	$450 \leqslant m < 475$	$475 \leqslant m < 500$
Frequency	18	25	28	13

a Estimate the range for this data.   **(1 mark)**

b Explain why the actual range of the data will differ from your answer to part **a**.   **(1 mark)**

c Calculate the 30% to 70% interpercentile range.   **(3 marks)**

d Estimate the number of kittens whose masses fall within the range you calculated in part **c**.   **(2 marks)**

P 6 The lengths of time customers are kept on hold at a company call centre are recorded in the table.

Time, t (mins)	$0 \leqslant t < 4$	$4 \leqslant t < 8$	$8 \leqslant t < 12$	$12 \leqslant t < 16$	$16 \leqslant t < 20$
Frequency	6	18	27	32	17

The company claims that 90% of customers wait between 2 and 16 minutes for their call to be answered. By calculating suitable percentiles, comment on the validity of the company's claim.   **(3 marks)**

2.4   Variance and standard deviation

1 The scores, marked out of 10, achieved by 6 students in a quiz are:

　　5　8　6　7　8　4

Find:

Hint Use the formula,
$$\text{variance} = \frac{\sum x^2}{n} - \left(\frac{\sum x}{n}\right)^2$$
The standard deviation is the square root of variance.

a the variance

b the standard deviation.

2 The table shows some grouped data.

x	0	1	2	3	4
f	4	8	9	17	6

Calculate:

a $\sum fx^2$ 　　　　　**b** the standard deviation.

Hint For part **b**, use the formula for standard deviation of grouped data
$$\sigma = \sqrt{\frac{\sum fx^2}{\sum f} - \left(\frac{\sum fx}{\sum f}\right)^2}$$
Alternatively, enter the values into your calculator.

3 The table shows the masses of children in a year 9 class.

Mass, m (kg)	Frequency
$35 \leqslant m < 40$	5
$40 \leqslant m < 45$	7
$45 \leqslant m < 50$	8
$50 \leqslant m < 55$	6
$55 \leqslant m < 60$	4

Calculate an estimate for:

a the variance 　　　　**b** the standard deviation.

Hint Use the midpoint of each class either in the formula given in the hint above, or as column 1 in a table on your calculator.

E/P 4 A keen gardener has many rose bushes. One day the gardener counts the number of ladybirds on each bush and records the data in a table.

Number of ladybirds	Frequency
5	11
6	15
7	23
8	16

a Use your calculator to work out the mean and standard deviation of the number of ladybirds on a rose bush. **(2 marks)**

The gardener repeats the count of ladybirds two weeks later and finds the mean number to be 7.1 and the standard deviation to be 0.94.

b Compare the data on the two days. **(2 marks)**

5 Jez is a postman. For each day in one working month he records the time it takes him, in hours, to complete his round.

Time, t (hours)	$4 \leqslant t < 4.5$	$4.5 \leqslant t < 5$	$5 \leqslant t < 5.5$	$5.5 \leqslant t < 6$	$6 \leqslant t < 6.5$
Frequency	5	7	8	3	1

    a Use your calculator to estimate the mean and standard deviation of the data. **(2 marks)**

Jez claims that he completes 80% of his rounds within one standard deviation of the mean time.

    b Comment on Jez's claim. **(2 marks)**

6 A set of 6 numbers has mean 5 and variance 7.
A second set of 5 numbers has mean 5.5 and variance 6.5.
Find the mean and variance of the combined set of 11 numbers. **(4 marks)**

7 From the large data set for Camborne in August 2015, the following summary statistics are collected for the daily mean temperature.

$$\sum x = 477.4 \qquad\qquad \sum x^2 = 7374.7$$

Find the standard deviation of the daily mean temperatures. **(2 marks)**

2.5 Coding

1 A set of data values, d, is shown below:

    60   70   80   40   50   80   70

    a Code the data using the coding $x = \dfrac{d}{10}$

    b Calculate the mean of the coded values, $\bar{x}$.

> **Hint** If $x = \dfrac{d}{10}$ then $\bar{x} = \dfrac{\bar{d}}{10}$

    c Use your answer to part **b** to calculate $\bar{d}$.

2 A set of data is coded using $y = 2x - 1$. It is found that $\bar{y} = 15$ and $\sigma_y = 6$.
Find:

    a the mean of the original data, $\bar{x}$

    b the standard deviation of the original data, σ_x

> **Hint** When data is coded using $y = px + q$, the standard deviation and variance are only affected by the value of p.

    c the variance of the original data.

3 The prices of packs of apples, x pence, in ten supermarkets are recorded.

The data is coded using $y = \dfrac{x - 20}{100}$ and the following summary statistics are obtained:

$$\sum y = 20 \qquad\qquad \sum y^2 = 48$$

Find:

    a the mean price of a pack of apples **(2 marks)**

    b the standard deviation of the prices of packs of apples. **(2 marks)**

(E) **4** A meteorologist records the daily mean pressures, p hPa, at Heathrow on the first 10 days of May 2015.

The data is coded using $x = \dfrac{p - 1000}{2}$. The summary statistics are:

$$\sum x = 43.5 \qquad\qquad \sum x^2 = 365.25$$

Find:

  a the mean of the daily mean pressures   **(2 marks)**

  b the variance of the daily mean pressures.   **(2 marks)**

(E/P) **5** Yvonne is investigating the salaries of top executives in the banking industry.

  a Given that a typical salary is in excess of £100 000, explain why it might be sensible for Yvonne to code her raw data.   **(1 mark)**

She records the salaries of 8 people and uses the coding $y = ax + b$ where x is the original data and y is the coded data. Her coded summary statistics are:

$$\sum y = 104 \qquad\qquad \sum y^2 = 1634$$

  b Given that the mean salary in the sample is £165 000 and the variance is 881 250 000, find the values of a and b.   **(3 marks)**

Problem solving   Set A

Bronze

The number of tracks on each of 11 albums is shown below:

    12   13   12   8   9   11   12   10   9   13   14

Calculate the interquartile range for this data.   **(2 marks)**

Silver

In a survey, a random sample of 140 people were asked how long they spent commuting to work every week, to the nearest hour. The results are recorded in the table.

Number of hours	Frequency
0–2	19
3–4	47
5–6	57
7–10	17

Use linear interpolation to find the interquartile range for this data.   **(3 marks)**

Gold

The table shows the scores achieved by 160 students in a mock examination.

Score, $x\%$	Frequency
$0 \leqslant x < 20$	12
$20 \leqslant x < 40$	31
$40 \leqslant x < 60$	58
$60 \leqslant x < 80$	44
$80 \leqslant x \leqslant 100$	15

a Use linear interpolation to find the 10th to 90th interpercentile range of this data. **(3 marks)**

The next year, 200 students will sit a similar mock examination. The school wants to set a pass mark such that 175 of these students will pass.

b Based on this year's mock examination scores, suggest a suitable pass mark. **(2 marks)**

c State one assumption you have made in your calculation in part **b**. **(1 mark)**

Problem solving Set B

Bronze

Stevo is a keen fisherman. Over the course of a year, he records the amount of time he spends fishing on each day he goes out. His results are summarised in the table.

Time, t (hours)	$2 \leqslant t < 3$	$3 \leqslant t < 4.5$	$4.5 \leqslant t < 5$	$5 \leqslant t < 7$	$7 \leqslant t < 10$
Frequency	18	40	51	36	62

a Estimate the mean and standard deviation for this data. **(2 marks)**

b Explain why your answers to part **a** are estimates. **(1 mark)**

Silver

Data is collected on the masses, m kg, of 140 Humboldt penguins.

Mass, m (kg)	$3 \leqslant m < 3.5$	$3.5 \leqslant m < k$	$k \leqslant m < 4.0$	$4.0 \leqslant m < 4.5$	$4.5 \leqslant m < 6$
Frequency	17	21	33	54	15

a Given that an estimate for the mean mass of the penguins is 4.09 kg, find the value of k. **(3 marks)**

b Calculate an estimate for the standard deviation. **(1 mark)**

c Explain why your answer to part **b** is an estimate. **(1 mark)**

Gold

The salaries of 50 employees in an IT company are recorded in the table.

Salary, £'000	Frequency
$10 \leqslant x < 12$	2
$12 \leqslant x < 15$	5
$15 \leqslant x < 20$	12
$20 \leqslant x < 25$	13
$25 \leqslant x < 30$	7
$30 \leqslant x < 50$	8
$50 \leqslant x$	3

The human resources manager wants to calculate an estimate for the mean salary.

a Identify one problem that the manager will have in calculating an estimate using the data given. **(1 mark)**

b Suggest a possible assumption that the manager could make to rectify this problem. **(1 mark)**

c Using your assumption in part **b**, calculate an estimate for the mean salary. **(2 marks)**

In reality, the mean salary was found to be £31 000.

d Comment on your assumption from part **b** in light of this information, and suggest a reason for any discrepancy. **(2 marks)**

Now try this → Exam question bank Q6, Q13, Q15, Q24, Q30

3.1   Outliers

1   The scores achieved by a group of students on a maths test are recorded.

The quartiles are: $Q_1 = 50\%$ and $Q_3 = 65\%$.
A value greater than $Q_3 + 1.5 \times (Q_3 - Q_1)$ or smaller than $Q_1 - 1.5 \times (Q_3 - Q_1)$ is defined as an outlier.

Work out whether the following scores are outliers, according to this definition:

Hint Use the definition of an outlier supplied in the question, and work out the lower and upper bounds.

a 12%   **b** 71%   **c** 90%

2   Some data is collected. The mean and standard deviation are calculated and found to be 14.5 and 6.2 respectively.

An outlier is defined as an observation which lies more than 2 standard deviations from the mean.

Hint There are many possible definitions of an outlier. You will be told which definition to use in the question.

Work out whether the following are outliers using this rule:

a 12.5   **b** 27.1   **c** 26.9

P 3   The lengths of a colony of rattlesnakes are recorded. The mean length is 1.5 m and the variance is 0.04.

An outlier is an observation which lies ±2 standard deviations from the mean.
The length of one of the rattlesnakes is recorded as 2.1 m.

a State, with a reason, whether this is an outlier.   **(2 marks)**

b Calculate the largest and smallest lengths that a rattlesnake can be without being considered an outlier.   **(2 marks)**

c State, with a reason, whether this recorded length should be removed from the data.   **(2 marks)**

P 4   The ages of 20 people on a coach trip are recorded. The lower quartile of the ages is found to be 22 and the upper quartile is found to be 46.

An outlier is an observation that falls either 1.5 × the interquartile range below the lower quartile, or 1.5 × the interquartile range above the upper quartile.

a Calculate the minimum age and maximum age a person on the trip could be without being considered an outlier.   **(3 marks)**

One of the people on the trip has an age recorded as 103.

b Suggest a reason why this could be a legitimate data value.   **(1 mark)**

E/P **5** The ages of 10 students at a secondary school are recorded.

The summary statistics are $\sum x = 154$ and $\sum x^2 = 2438$.

    a Calculate the mean and standard deviation of the ages. **(3 marks)**

An outlier is an observation which lies ± 2 standard deviations from the mean.
One of the ages recorded is 21.

    b State, with a reason, whether this is an outlier. **(2 marks)**

Poppy decides to exclude this data value from her analysis.

    c Give one reason to justify this decision. **(1 mark)**

    d Calculate the mean and standard deviation of the 9 remaining students. **(3 marks)**

E/P **6** The daily mean temperatures, °C, are recorded for a random sample of 12 days in Beijing.

    18.5   26.1   27.4   27.9   28.1   28.2   29.4   30.9   30.4   27.2   30.0   42.6

    a Calculate the mean and standard deviation of the daily mean temperatures. **(2 marks)**

An outlier is an observation which is ± 2 standard deviations from the mean.

    b Show that there are two outliers in the data and state their values. **(2 marks)**

    c Suggest, with reasons, whether the outliers should be excluded from the data. **(2 marks)**

    d Clean the data and recalculate the mean and standard deviation. **(2 marks)**

3.2 Box plots

1 A group of learner drivers took a test in which they had to identify road hazards.

Their scores are summarised as follows:

    Lower quartile = 30   Median = 42   Upper quartile = 45
    Lowest score = 18   Highest score = 52

Given that there are no outliers, draw a box plot to illustrate this data.

> **Hint** Draw little vertical lines at each key value from the summary data.

2 The diagram shows a box plot of the goals scored by football teams over a season.

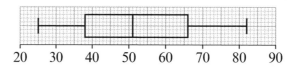

Write down:

    a the median   **b** the interquartile range

    c the range.

> **Hint** Read the quartiles and maximum and minimum values from the box plot.

P **3** The masses, in grams, of a group of male and female ruby-throated hummingbirds are recorded. The data is summarised in two box plots.

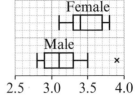

a Explain what is represented by × in the box plot for the male hummingbirds. **(1 mark)**

b Compare the masses of the male and female hummingbirds. **(2 marks)**

One of the hummingbirds is found to have a mass of 3.6 g.

c State, with a reason, whether this hummingbird is likely to be male or female. **(1 mark)**

P **4** Data for the daily mean windspeed (in knots) in Leuchars is July 1987 is taken from the large data set.

3	4	5	5	5	5	5	5	5	5	6
6	6	7	7	7	8	8	8	8	9	9
9	9	10	11	11	12	15	16	19		

a Calculate the median and the interquartile range. **(3 marks)**

An outlier is defined as a value which lies either 1.5 × the interquartile range above the upper quartile or 1.5 × the interquartile range below the lower quartile.

b Determine whether there are any outliers in the data. **(2 marks)**

c Draw a box plot for this data. **(3 marks)**

3.3 Cumulative frequency

1 The table shows the heights, in cm, of 70 teenagers.

Height, h (cm)	$130 \leqslant h < 140$	$140 \leqslant h < 150$	$150 \leqslant h < 160$	$160 \leqslant h < 170$
Frequency	15	18	23	14

a Draw a cumulative frequency table for this data.

> **Hint** Add up the frequencies as you go along.

b Draw a cumulative frequency diagram for this data.

> **Hint** Each point is plotted at the upper class boundary.

2 The cumulative frequency diagram shows the masses, in grams, of 120 apples.

Find an estimate for:

> **Hint** Draw horizontal lines across to the curve from the cumulative frequency axis.

a the median mass

b the interquartile range.

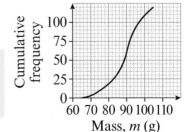

19

E **3** The cumulative frequency diagram shows the times taken, in minutes, by a number of fun runners to complete an obstacle course.

a State how many runners took part. **(1 mark)**

b Estimate the median time taken. **(2 marks)**

The qualifying time for the regional final was 58 minutes.

c Estimate the number of runners who qualified for the regional final. **(2 marks)**

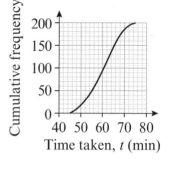

E/P **4** From the large data set, the daily mean temperature (°C) in Hurn for the months of May and June 2015 is summarised in the cumulative frequency diagram.

a Write down the number of days represented in this cumulative frequency diagram **(1 mark)**

b Estimate the median and interquartile range of the daily mean temperatures. **(3 marks)**

c Estimate the number of days during this period that the temperature was greater than 15 °C. **(2 marks)**

Phyllis says that the range of temperatures for the given period is 12 °C.

d Explain why Phyllis might be wrong. **(2 marks)**

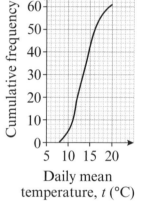

E/P **5** The masses, in grams, of a crop of potatoes are shown in the cumulative frequency diagram.

Only potatoes weighing between 102 g and 117 g can be sold to a supermarket.
Estimate the percentage of the crop that can be sold to the supermarket. **(4 marks)**

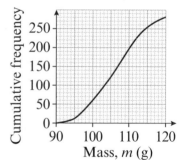

 3.4 **Histograms**

1 The table records the times taken by a group of Sudoku enthusiasts to complete a puzzle.

Time, t (min)	$3 \leqslant t < 4$	$4 \leqslant t < 4.5$	$4.5 \leqslant t < 5$	$5 \leqslant t < 6.5$	$6.5 \leqslant t < 8$
Frequency	7	13	19	15	6

a Write down the class width of the $4 \leqslant t < 4.5$ interval.

b Calculate the frequency densities for each class.

Hint frequency density $= \dfrac{\text{frequency}}{\text{class width}}$

2 The table shows the length of time, *t* minutes, that it takes 41 cats to eat their dinner.

Time, *t* (min)	$0 \leqslant t < 3$	$3 \leqslant t < 4$	$4 \leqslant t < 4.5$	$4.5 \leqslant t < 5$	$5 \leqslant t < 6$	$6 \leqslant t < 10$
Frequency	3	6	8	7	5	12

a Explain why a histogram is a suitable diagram for displaying this data.

b Draw a histogram to represent the data.

> **Hint** Calculate the frequency densities first.

P 3 The table shows the lengths of time, to the nearest ms, that it takes a group of students to respond to a stimulus.

Time, *t* (ms)	$0 \leqslant t < 4$	$4 \leqslant t < 6$	$6 \leqslant t < 7$	$7 \leqslant t < 7.5$	$7.5 \leqslant t < 8.5$	$8.5 \leqslant t < 10$
Frequency	2	10	15	12	8	3

a Give two reasons why a histogram is appropriate for displaying this data. **(2 marks)**

The bar to represent the students who took between 4 ms and 6 ms to respond is of width 1 cm and height 2.5 cm.

b Calculate the width and height of the bar representing students who took between 7.5 ms and 8.5 ms to respond. **(4 marks)**

P 4 The histogram shows the distribution of the heights of 66 garden gnomes in a garden centre.

a Write down the number of gnomes that are between 25 cm and 35 cm tall. **(2 marks)**

A gnome collector wants to buy all of the gnomes that are greater than 45 cm tall.

b Calculate the percentage of the 66 gnomes that the collector will buy. **(3 marks)**

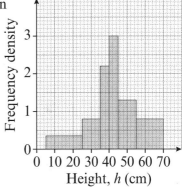

P 5 The table shows the times taken, in minutes, by runners to complete a cross-country race.

Time, *t* (min)	$35 \leqslant t < 45$	$45 \leqslant t < 50$	$50 \leqslant t < 55$	$55 \leqslant t < 65$	$65 \leqslant t < 100$
Frequency	18	*p*	42	*q*	14

The partially completed histogram shows the same data.

a Calculate the values of *p* and *q*. **(3 marks)**

b Calculate the height of the bar representing runners who took between 50 and 55 minutes to complete the race. **(2 marks)**

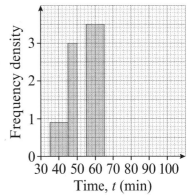

E/P **6** The histogram shows the masses, in kg, of 200 Malabar large-spotted civets.

Use interpolation to estimate the number of civets that are heavier than 10 kg. **(4 marks)**

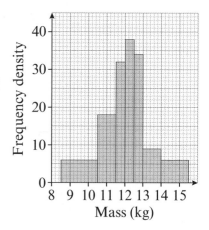

3.5 Comparing data

1 Summary statistics are calculated for the daily total hours of sunshine in a random sample taken from each of Hurn and Leeming during 1987. The results are shown in the table.

	Median	**Interquartile range**
Hurn	4.1 hours	5.6 hours
Leeming	4.9 hours	4.2 hours

© Crown Copyright Met Office

Write down two comparisons between the data from the two locations.

Hint Compare a measure of location and a measure of spread.

Give your answers in the context of the data.

2 The times taken, in minutes, to complete a Kakuro puzzle are recorded for a random sample of year 8 students and a random sample of year 10 students. Summary statistics for each of the two data sets are recorded in the table.

	n	$\sum x$	$\sum x^2$
Year 8	15	94	610
Year 10	10	79	688

a Calculate the mean and standard deviation of each data set.

b Compare the two data sets.

Hint Make sure you give two comparisons.

P 3 The box plots show the distributions of daily mean windspeeds in Camborne and Leuchars during July and August 2015.

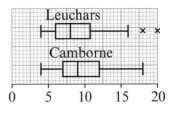

Anne and Colin want to go on a sailing holiday. To get the best out of the holiday, they want the windspeed to be as consistent as possible.

a Suggest, with reasons, which of the two locations they should go to for their holiday. **(2 marks)**

These box plots show the data on daily maximum gusts in Camborne and Leuchars for the same two months.

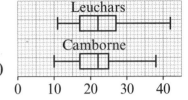

b Does this information change your recommendation? Give a reason for your answer. **(2 marks)**

E 4 The cumulative frequency diagram shows the distribution of lengths in cm of 50 male and 50 female Eurasian otters.

Compare the lengths of male and female otters. **(4 marks)**

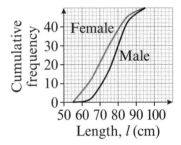

P 5 A rodent expert records the masses, in grams, of colonies of brown and black rats. Her results are shown in the table.

Mass (g)	Frequency (black rats)	Frequency (brown rats)
$100 \leqslant m < 150$	2	1
$150 \leqslant m < 200$	7	8
$200 \leqslant m < 250$	18	32
$250 \leqslant m < 300$	24	22
$300 \leqslant m < 350$	13	7
$350 \leqslant m < 400$	6	0

a Draw cumulative frequency diagrams for both sets of data on the same axes. **(3 marks)**

b State which type of rat has the greater spread of masses. **(2 marks)**

A black rat is considered overweight if its mass is greater than 320 g and a brown rat is considered overweight if its mass is greater than 280 g.

c Which colony contains the greatest number of overweight rats? **(2 marks)**

Set A

Bronze

The times taken, t seconds, for each of ten dogs to eat a biscuit are recorded.

The following summary statistics are calculated:

$$\sum t = 42 \qquad \sum t^2 = 216.4$$

An outlier is defined as being a data point that is greater than ±2 standard deviations from the mean.

One of the dogs took 8.3 seconds to eat a biscuit.

a Show that this piece of data is an outlier. **(3 marks)**

A student decides to remove this time from the data set before analysing the data further.

b Suggest one reason why this may not be a valid approach. **(1 mark)**

Silver

A supermarket is testing the masses, m grams, of grapefruit. The masses of a random sample of 20 grapefruits are recorded, and the data is summarised as follows:

$$n = 20 \qquad \sum m = 3218 \qquad \sum m^2 = 530\,276$$

An outlier is defined as being a data point that is greater than ±2 standard deviations from the mean.

The two largest masses recorded in the sample are 223 g and 845 g.

Benedict suggests that both of these values should be removed from the data set.

Use the definition of an outlier given above to evaluate Benedict's suggestion. **(4 marks)**

Gold

A chemical reaction is carried out 9 times. Each time the volume of reactant, in ml, is recorded. The results are shown below:

13　43　25　29　51　36　75　52　27

A researcher wants to identify extreme data values before carrying out her analysis. To do this, she proposes two different definitions of an outlier.

Definition A: a data point that is greater than ±2 standard deviations from the mean.

Definition B: a data point that is more than 1.5 × the interquartile range below the lower quartile, or is more than 1.5 × the interquartile range above the upper quartile.

State, with reasons, which of these definitions would be most useful to the researcher.

(5 marks)

Problem solving Set B

Bronze

The histogram shows the times taken, in minutes, for a group of 600 students to complete a jigsaw puzzle.

Estimate the number of students who took between 32 and 42 minutes to complete the puzzle. **(4 marks)**

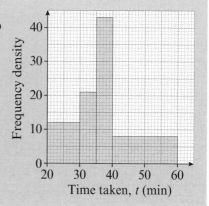

Silver

The histogram shows the times taken, in minutes, for a group of 100 runners to complete a cross-country race.

Estimate the number of runners who took between 25 and 50 minutes to complete the race. **(4 marks)**

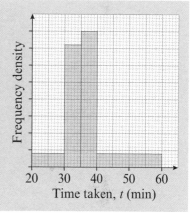

Gold

A group of 120 swimmers completed an open water race and recorded their finishing times, t minutes. The times for two thirds of the participants are shown on the histogram. The bars for $30 \leqslant t < 35$ and $40 \leqslant t < 45$ are missing.

Four times as many swimmers finished the race in 40–45 minutes as finished the race in 30–35 minutes.

Estimate the number of swimmers who took between 25 and 43 minutes to complete the race. **(6 marks)**

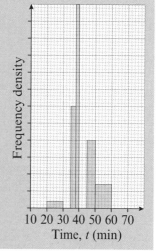

Now try this → **Exam question bank Q11, Q20, Q22, Q26, Q36**

4 Correlation

4.1 Correlation

1 State the type of correlation shown by each of these scatter diagrams.

Hint Look for a pattern in the data.

a

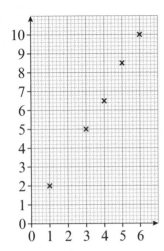

b

c

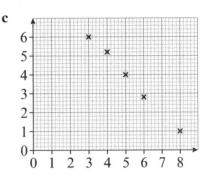

2 The table shows the results of an experiment.

x	10.1	9.6	8.2	7.4	6.1	5.8	4.1	3.7	3.1	2.5
y	1.2	2.3	3.7	4.5	4.9	4.3	5.9	6.1	6.5	8.1

a Draw a scatter diagram for this data.

b Describe the type of correlation shown.

Hint Plot the bivariate data points as coordinates.

(E) 3 The daily mean temperatures, $x\,°C$, and the daily total sunshine, y hours, were recorded on 7 days in one month in 1987 in Camborne.
The scatter diagram shows this data.

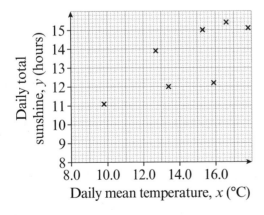

a Describe the type of correlation shown by the scatter diagram. **(1 mark)**

b Interpret the correlation in context. **(1 mark)**

c Using your knowledge of the large data set, state which month these data might have been sampled from. **(1 mark)**

E/P **4** The engine sizes in litres and the numbers of miles per gallon are recorded for seven cars.

Engine size (litres)	1.1	1.3	1.4	1.6	1.8	2.0	2.4
Miles per gallon	58	52	49	45	42	40	32

    a Draw a scatter diagram for this data. **(3 marks)**

    b Describe and interpret the correlation between the two variables. **(2 marks)**

    c State, with a reason, whether it is reasonable to conclude that there is a causal relationship between engine size and mileage. **(1 mark)**

E/P **5** Lenaee is a keen follower of Straston Town Football Club. She collects data on the crowd attendance, in thousands, at seven home games and records the total number of goals scored in each match. She displays this information in a scatter diagram.

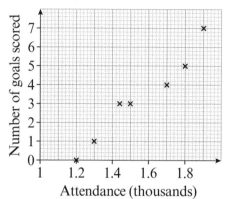

    a Describe the correlation shown in the scatter diagram. **(1 mark)**

Lenaee says that there is a causal relationship between the size of the crowd and the total number of goals scored.

    b Comment on Lenaee's claim. **(2 marks)**

E/P **6** The table shows the daily mean visibilities, v Dm, and the daily mean pressures, p hPa, in Leeming for a random sample of 10 days in July 2015.

Daily mean visibility, v	1100	2800	2900	2800	2600	3300	3500	3200	3300	3600
Daily mean pressure, p	1004	1007	1007	1007	1008	1011	1013	1013	1013	1015

© Crown Copyright Met Office

The median and quartiles for the visibility data are:

$$Q_1 = 2800 \qquad Q_2 = 3050 \qquad Q_3 = 3300$$

An outlier is defined as a value which lies either more than 1.5 × the interquartile range above the upper quartile or more than 1.5 × the interquartile range below the lower quartile.

    a Show that $v = 1100$ is an outlier. **(1 mark)**

    b Give a reason why you might:

      i include   **ii** exclude this day's readings. **(2 marks)**

    c Exclude the day's readings and draw a scatter diagram to represent the data for the remaining nine days. **(3 marks)**

    d Describe the correlation between daily mean visibility and daily mean pressure. **(1 mark)**

    e Using your knowledge of the large data set, explain whether there could be a causal relationship between the daily mean visibility and the daily mean pressure. **(1 mark)**

4.2 Linear regression

1 Three scatter diagrams are shown below.

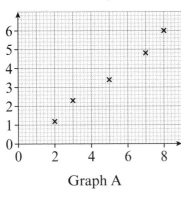
Graph A

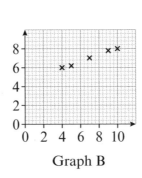
Graph B

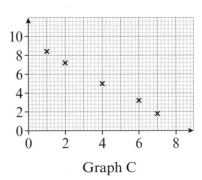
Graph C

Match the regression equations to the graphs.

a $y = 0.75x - 0.19$ **b** $y = 9.30 - 1.05x$

c $y = 0.35x + 4.60$

Hint Consider the gradients and y-intercepts of the lines of best fit.

2 It is known that cola can erode a copper coin. A newly minted 1p coin has mass 3.56 g. Hannah decides to immerse the new coin in cola and record its mass, x grams, after t hours. She finds that the equation of the regression line of x on t for her data is $x = 3.56 - 0.012t$. For the regression equation, interpret the meaning of the values:

Hint The regression line shows the trend over time.

a 3.56   **b** −0.012

(E/P) 3 Sanjeevan collects data on the value, y £1000s, of office blocks in the business district of his local town, and on the number of offices, x, within those office blocks. He calculates the equation of the regression line for y on x to be $y = 50 + 20x$.

  a Use Sanjeevan's regression line to find an estimate for the value of an office block with 12 offices. **(1 mark)**

  b Interpret the meaning of the number 20, the coefficient of x, in the equation. **(1 mark)**

Sanjeevan claims that the value of a building in the business district with no offices is £50 000.

  c State, with a reason, whether this is likely to be the case. **(2 marks)**

(E/P) 4 Scarlett is a zoologist and collects data on the masses, x g, of Siberian chipmunks, t days after they are born. The data is shown in the table.

Days after birth, t	1	2	4	6	7	8	10
Mass of chipmunk, x (g)	7.5	12	21	30	34.5	39	48

She calculates the equation of the regression line of x on t to be $x = 3 + 4.5t$.

  a Interpret the meaning of the values 3 and 4.5 in the regression equation. **(2 marks)**

  b Explain why it would not be sensible to use the regression line to predict the mass of a chipmunk that is 30 days old. **(1 mark)**

  c Explain why it would not be appropriate to use the regression line to predict the number of days after birth for a chipmunk weighing 32 g. **(1 mark)**

E/P **5** The daily mean temperatures, $x\,°C$, and the daily mean pressures, $y\,$hPa, are recorded for a random sample of 10 days in Beijing in June 2015. The data is displayed in a scatter diagram.

The equation of the regression line of y on x is calculated to be $y = 1043 - 1.41x$.

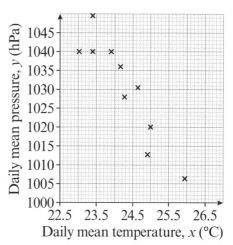

a Comment on the validity of using the regression line to estimate the daily mean pressure when the daily mean temperature is:

   i 24.5 °C   **ii** 28.2 °C   **(2 marks)**

b Explain why it would not be appropriate to use the regression line to predict the daily mean temperature when the daily mean pressure is 1009 hPa. **(1 mark)**

c With reference to correlation, comment on how accurately the regression model reflects the data. **(2 marks)**

Problem solving

Bronze

Some meteorologists are interested in the relationship between the daily minimum temperature, $x\,°C$, and the daily maximum temperature, $y\,°C$, in a particular town. They take a random sample of 7 days and record the data in a table.

Minimum temperature, x (°C)	0.6	1.1	1.7	2.8	3.3	5.0	7.2
Maximum temperature, y (°C)	12.2	13.9	14.4	16.7	17.2	19.4	22.2

a Draw a scatter diagram to represent this data. **(2 marks)**

b Explain why a linear regression model may be appropriate to describe the relationship between the daily minimum temperature and the daily maximum temperature. **(1 mark)**

c Suggest, with a reason, whether it would be sensible to use the regression model to predict the daily maximum temperature when the daily minimum temperature is 12 °C. **(1 mark)**

Silver

A survey of 10 two-bedroom flats in a particular town is carried out. The value of the flats, y £1000s, and the distance, x km, from the town centre is recorded.

A scatter diagram is drawn to show the data.

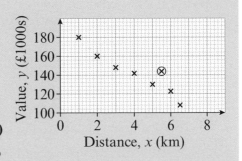

a Give a reason to support the use of linear regression to model this data. **(1 mark)**

The equation of the regression line of y on x is found to be $y = 185 - 10x$.

b Interpret the values 185 and −10 in the regression equation. **(2 marks)**

c Explain why it would not be sensible to use the regression model to find y when $x = 11$. **(1 mark)**

The point representing one of the flats has been circled on the graph.

d State, with a reason, whether you think this point is likely to represent a recording error or a valid data value. **(1 mark)**

Gold

A researcher is investigating the link between humidity and visibility using the large data set. The researcher analyses the data for Heathrow in 2015, and considers the daily maximum relative humidity, $x\%$, and the daily mean visibility, y 100 Dm, for each day.

The equation of the regression line for y on x is found to be $y = 113 - 0.933x$.

a Give an interpretation of the value −0.933 in the regression equation. **(1 mark)**

b Using your knowledge of the large data set, suggest, with a reason, whether it would be sensible to use this regression model to estimate the mean visibility on a day when the daily maximum relative humidity is:

i 90% ii 40% **(2 marks)**

c Using your knowledge of the large data set, explain whether there could be a causal relationship between these variables. **(1 mark)**

d Explain why it would not be appropriate to use the regression line to find the humidity on a day when the visibility is 3500 Dm. **(1 mark)**

Now try this → Exam question bank Q4, Q8, Q12, Q19, Q21

5.1 Calculating probabilities

1 One letter is chosen at random from the word INTERPOLATION.

> **Hint** Count the number of successful outcomes in each case.

Calculate the probability that the letter is:

a an N   **b** a vowel   **c** before Q in the alphabet.

2 A fair six-sided dice is thrown at the same time as a fair four-sided dice.

> **Hint** You can draw a sample space diagram showing all the possible outcomes.

Calculate the probability that the product of the scores on the two dice is:

a 15   **b** even   **c** greater than 10.

E/P 3 The heights, h cm, of a group of volleyball players are recorded in the table.

Height, h (cm)	$150 \leqslant h < 160$	$160 \leqslant h < 170$	$170 \leqslant h < 180$	$180 \leqslant h < 190$	$190 \leqslant h < 200$
Frequency	7	22	35	16	9

One player is chosen at random.

a Find the probability that the player is less than 180 cm tall. **(2 marks)**

b Estimate the probability that the player is greater than 178 cm tall. **(2 marks)**

c State one assumption you have made in calculating your answer to part **b**. **(1 mark)**

E/P 4 The histogram shows the masses, m kg, of 60 adult male warthogs.

One warthog is chosen at random.

a Find the probability that the warthog has a mass less than 90 kg. **(2 marks)**

b Estimate the probability that the warthog has a mass greater than 110 kg. **(3 marks)**

c State an assumption you have made in calculating your answer to part **b**. **(1 mark)**

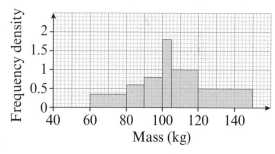

E/P 5 Myra and Nisha have two sets of cards. Set A has the letters B, E, and O printed on them. Set B has the numbers 4, 5, 6 and 7 printed on them. The cards are all face down.

Myra takes one card at random from each set.

a Write down all of Myra's possible outcomes. **(1 mark)**

b Find the probability that Myra selects:

  i the letter B and the number 4   **ii** a vowel and an even number. **(2 marks)**

Nisha takes two cards, at random, from set B.

c Write down all of Nisha's possible outcomes. **(1 mark)**

d Find the probability that Nisha selects:

  i two odd numbers   **ii** two numbers with a total less than 12. **(2 marks)**

5.2 Venn diagrams

1 Calculate:

   a P(A)   **b** P(A and B)

   c P(A or B).

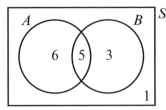

Hint Calculate the total of all the numbers in the Venn diagram.

2 A group of 20 students are asked if they like tapioca or semolina: 9 students said they liked tapioca, 14 students said they liked semolina, and 5 students said they liked both.

Draw a Venn diagram to illustrate this information.

Hint Calculate the number of students who liked only tapioca and only semolina.

3 Two events A and B have associated probabilities:

P(A and B) = 0.2
P(not A and not B) = 0.5
P(A but not B) = 2 × P(B but not A)

Calculate P(A but not B).

Hint Draw a Venn diagram like this, and use the fact that all the probabilities in the sample space must add up to 1.

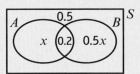

(E/P) 4 A passenger on an aeroplane watches a movie with probability 0.8 and a nature documentary with probability 0.3. The probability that the passenger watches either one or both of these options is 0.9.

Find the probability that the passenger watches:

   a both the movie and the nature documentary   **(2 marks)**

   b the nature documentary but not the movie.   **(2 marks)**

(E/P) 5 The Venn diagram shows the probabilities of chickens in a farmyard doing various things in a given period of time.

   A represents the event that the chicken pecks.
   B represents the event that the chicken clucks.
   C represents the event that the chicken lays an egg.

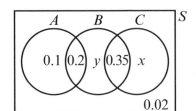

Given that P(C) = 0.5,

   a find x **(1 mark)**

   b find y.   **(2 marks)**

E/P **6** A group of 70 circus performers are asked if they juggle, ride a unicycle or eat fire:

2 performers say that they do all three things
17 performers juggle and ride a unicycle
8 performers ride a unicycle and eat fire
12 performers juggle and eat fire
30 performers juggle
32 performers ride a unicycle
25 performers eat fire

One performer is chosen at random.

Calculate the probability that the performer:

a juggles **(1 mark)**

b juggles or rides a unicycle, or both **(2 marks)**

c only eats fire **(2 marks)**

d does none of the three things. **(2 marks)**

E/P **7** The Venn diagram shows the probabilities of members of an athletics club taking part in various events.

A represents the event that the member takes part in the javelin.
B represents the event that the member takes part in the discus.
C represents the event that the member takes part in the shot put.

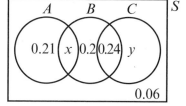

a Given that P(*B*) = 0.62, find the values of *x* and *y*. **(3 marks)**

b Calculate the probability that a member chosen at random takes part in either the javelin or the shot put, but not the discus. **(2 marks)**

E/P **8** The Venn diagram shows the number of children at a party who like different types of pudding.

A represents the event that the child likes jelly.
B represents the event that the child likes ice cream.
C represents the event that the child likes blancmange.

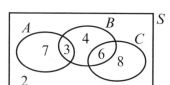

One of the children is chosen at random.

a Show that the probability that the child likes more than one type of pudding is $\frac{3}{10}$

(2 marks)

b Find the probability that the child likes jelly, or ice cream, or both. **(2 marks)**

c Write down the probability that the child likes both ice cream and blancmange. **(1 mark)**

5.3 Mutually exclusive and independent events

1 Events *A* and *B* are mutually exclusive, and P(*A*) = 0.3 and P(*B*) = 0.45.

Hint Draw a Venn diagram.

  a Find P(*A* or *B*).   **b** Find P(neither *A* nor *B*).

2 Events *A* and *B* are mutually exclusive, and P(*A* or *B*) = 0.7 and P(*B*) = 0.5.

Hint If two events are mutually exclusive, P(*A* and *B*) = 0.

  a Find P(*A*).   **b** Find P(neither *A* nor *B*).

3 P(*A*) = 0.6 and P(*B*) = 0.4.

Given that events *A* and *B* are independent, find P(*A* and *B*).

Hint If two events are independent, you can multiply their probabilities to find the probability of both events happening.

4 P(*A*) = 0.12 and P(*A* and *B*) = 0.0204.

Given that events *A* and *B* are independent, find P(*B*).

Hint You can rearrange the formula for the multiplication rule for independent events.

(E/P) 5 The Venn diagram shows the probabilities that a cat likes *Lixilike* cat food (*A*) or *Purrfect* cat food (*B*).

  a Write down the value of *x*. **(1 mark)**

  b Determine whether the events 'likes *Lixilike*' and 'likes *Purrfect*' are independent. **(3 marks)**

(E/P) 6 *Y* and *Z* are two events such that P(*Y*) = 0.4, P(*Y* and not *Z*) = 0.15 and P(neither *Y* nor *Z*) = 0.35.

Show that events *Y* and *Z* are not independent. **(3 marks)**

(E/P) 7 The Venn diagram shows the probabilities of a group of students participating in various activities.

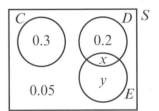

C represents taking part in school council.
D represents taking part in the school drama production.
E represents taking part in the Duke of Edinburgh scheme.

The probability that a student takes part in school council or the drama production is 0.65.

  a Write down two events that are mutually exclusive. **(1 mark)**

  b Find the value of *x* and the value of *y*. **(2 marks)**

A student claims that events *D* and *E* are independent.

  c Assess the student's claim. **(3 marks)**

8 Frank, Gracie and Igor sometimes miss their train to work.

F represents the event that Frank misses his train.
G represents the event that Gracie misses her train.
I represents the event that Igor misses his train.

The Venn diagram shows the three events, *F*, *G* and *I* and the probabilities associated with each region of event *G*. The constants *x*, *y* and *z* each represent probabilities associated with the three separate regions outside *G*.

a Write down two of the events that are mutually exclusive. Give a reason for your answer.
(1 mark)

The probability that Frank misses his train is 0.3.
The events *G* and *I* are independent.

b Find the values of *x*, *y* and *z*.
(4 marks)

5.4 Tree diagrams

1 A bag contains four red counters and five yellow counters. A counter is chosen at random, the colour is recorded and the counter is replaced.

A second counter is then chosen at random and the colour is recorded.

a Draw a tree diagram to show all the possible outcomes from this experiment.

b Calculate the probability that:

   i both counters are red

   ii only one counter is red.

> **Hint** Multiply probabilities along each branch and add up the probabilities for all the successful outcomes.

2 In a raffle game, a cup contains 15 tickets numbered from 1 to 15. A player gets to draw two tickets from the cup at random. The player wins a prize for each ticket that is a multiple of 5.

a Draw a tree diagram to show all the possible outcomes of both draws.

> **Hint** The first ticket is not replaced, so the probabilities will change for the second draw.

b Calculate the probability that:

   i the player chooses two winning tickets

   ii the player chooses exactly one winning ticket.

 3 The probability that a coach driver takes the motorway is 0.4. If the coach driver takes the motorway, the probability that the coach arrives on time at its destination is 0.9. If the driver does not take the motorway, the probability that the coach arrives on time at its destination is 0.3.

a Draw a tree diagram to represent this information. **(3 marks)**

b State, with a reason, whether the events 'takes the motorway' and 'arrives on time' are independent. **(1 mark)**

c Calculate the probability that the coach does not arrive on time at its destination. **(3 marks)**

E/P **4** In an experiment, a biased dice is rolled three times and it is recorded whether it lands on an odd number or not. P(odd) = 0.6.

By drawing a tree diagram, or otherwise, calculate the probability that:

a all three rolls are odd **(2 marks)**

b just one of the three rolls is odd. **(3 marks)**

The experiment is repeated twice more.

c Find the probability of obtaining either 3 odd numbers or 3 even numbers all three times. **(3 marks)**

E/P **5** A group of patients with a particular disease took part in a study to test three different medications. In the study, 20% of the patients were given medication A, 50% of the patients were given medication B, and the rest of the patients were given medication C.

The researchers found that 6% of the patients in the study were not cured. Given that 5% of the patients who received medication A were not cured and 7% of the patients who received medication B were not cured,

a find the percentage of patients who received medication C who were not cured. **(3 marks)**

A patient is chosen at random.

b Explain why the event 'the patient was given medication B' and the event 'the patient was not cured' are not statistically independent. **(1 mark)**

E/P **6** Two bags contain coloured balls. Bag A contains 7 balls, of which 4 are green and 3 are blue. Bag B contains 8 balls, of which 3 are green and 5 are blue.

A ball is drawn at random from bag A and placed into bag B. A second ball is then drawn a random from bag A and placed into bag B.

A third ball is then drawn at random from the 10 balls in bag B.

The event Q occurs when the two balls drawn from bag A are the same colour.

The event R occurs when the ball drawn from bag B is blue.

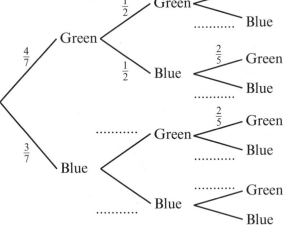

a Copy and complete the tree diagram shown above. **(4 marks)**

b Find P(Q). **(2 marks)**

c Show that P(R) = $\frac{41}{70}$ **(3 marks)**

d Hence write down the value of P(Q and R). **(1 mark)**

e State, with a reason, whether events Q and R are independent. **(1 mark)**

Problem solving — Set A

Bronze

A group of students are interviewed to find the types of food they like.

Event A is 'likes salad', event B is 'likes pasta' and event C is 'likes curry'.

One of these students is chosen at random, and a Venn diagram is drawn to show the probabilities of each outcome.

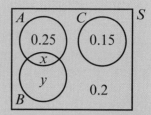

a Given that $P(A) = 0.55$, find the values of x and y. **(2 marks)**

b Show that events A and B are not statistically independent. **(2 marks)**

Silver

The Venn diagram shows the probabilities of two events, C and D.

a Given that events C and D are independent show that
$2x^2 - 0.68x - 0.0672 = 0$ **(3 marks)**

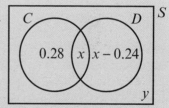

b Solve this quadratic equation, and hence find the values of x and y. **(3 marks)**

c Explain briefly why only one solution to the quadratic equation in part **a** should be considered. **(1 mark)**

Gold

The Venn diagram shows the probabilities of two events, A and B.
Given that events A and B are independent, find the values of x and y. **(4 marks)**

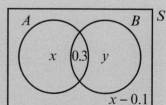

Problem solving — Set B

Bronze

A bag contains 6 orange tokens and 3 green tokens. A token is drawn out of the bag at random, the colour noted, and then replaced. A second token is then drawn out and the colour noted.

a Draw a tree diagram to illustrate this situation. **(3 marks)**

b Calculate the probability that one token of each colour is drawn. **(2 marks)**

Silver

A box contains 6 red counters, 3 green counters and 2 yellow counters. A counter is drawn out of the box at random. The colour is recorded and the counter is not replaced. A second counter is then drawn out and the colour is recorded.

a Draw a tree diagram to illustrate this situation. **(3 marks)**

b Calculate the probability that the counters are the same colour. **(2 marks)**

Gold

A box contains 8 ginger biscuits and 7 oat biscuits. Mathew chooses a biscuit at random. If it is a ginger biscuit, he puts it back. If it is an oat biscuit, he eats it. In either case, he then chooses a second biscuit. Again, if it is a ginger biscuit, he puts it back and if it is an oat biscuit, he eats it. He makes a third selection, with the same outcomes.

Find the probability that Mathew eats exactly two oat biscuits. **(4 marks)**

Now try this → **Exam question bank Q5, Q10, Q25, Q32, Q35**

6.1 Probability distributions

1 Write down, with a reason, whether or not each of the following is a discrete random variable.

Hint A discrete random variable can randomly take any of a specified range of discrete possible numerical outcomes.

   a The number, X, which shows uppermost when a fair six-sided dice is rolled.

   b The reaction time, T ms, recorded by a participant in an experiment.

   c The number of hours, H, in a day.

2 A fair six-sided dice is rolled. The number the dice lands on, X, is recorded.

Write the probability distribution of X as:

Hint Write down the probability of each of the outcomes in a table, or in the form $P(X = x) = k$.

   a a table   **b** a probability mass function.

Geena says that this distribution is an example of a discrete uniform distribution.

   c Explain what is meant by discrete uniform distribution.

3 A discrete random variable, Y, is modelled using the probability mass function

$$P(Y = y) = \frac{y}{k}, y = 1, 2, 3$$

Hint The sum of all probabilities should equal 1.

   a Find the value of k.

   b Write down the probability distribution of Y in table form.

   c Find the probability that:

     i $Y > 1$ **ii** $Y > 3$

4 A discrete random variable X has the probability distribution shown in the table.

x	1	2	3	4	5	6
$P(X = x)$	0.1	0.15	0.12	0.2	0.22	0.21

Find the probability that:

   a $X \leqslant 2$ **b** $X > 3$

   c $2 \leqslant X < 6$

Hint Work out which of the outcomes are included in each inequality.

(E) 5 The random variable, X, has probability function

$$P(X = x) = kx, x = 1, 2, 3, 4, 5$$

   a Show that $k = \frac{1}{15}$ **(2 marks)**

   b Find $P(X > 2)$.   **(2 marks)**

E/P 6 The table shows the probability distribution of a discrete random variable, Y.

y	1	2	3	4
$P(Y = y)$	$\alpha + \frac{1}{6}$	$\alpha - \frac{1}{8}$	α	2α

    a Find the value of α. **(2 marks)**

    b Find $P(1 < Y < 4)$. **(2 marks)**

E/P 7 A random number generator can generate any integer value from 1 to 20 with equal probability. Given that X is the random variable representing the number generated,

    a write down the name of the distribution of X. **(1 mark)**

    b Find:

        i $P(X > 15)$ **ii** $P(2 \leqslant X \leqslant 17)$ **(2 marks)**

    Two random numbers are generated.

    c Find the probability that they are both less than 10. **(3 marks)**

E/P 8 Mariah has a biased four-sided dice that can land on one of the numbers 1, 2, 3 or 4.

    The random variable X represents the number the dice lands on after a single roll.

    $P(X = r) = P(X = 5 - r)$ for $r = 1, 2$

    a Given that $P(X = 1) = 0.28$, find, in table form, the complete distribution of X. **(2 marks)**

    The dice is rolled twice and the totals are added together.

    b Find the probability that the total is 7 or more. **(3 marks)**

E/P 9 A fair seven-sided spinner is spun until it lands on green (G) or it has been spun five times in total.

Find the probability distribution of the random variable X, which represents the number of times the spinner is spun. **(4 marks)**

6.2 The binomial distribution

1 Write down, with reasons, whether or not each of the following situations can be modelled using a binomial distribution.

    a The number of heads obtained in 30 tosses of a fair coin.

    b The number of rolls of a fair dice that are needed to obtain a 6.

    c The number of wins achieved by a football team in a total of 20 matches played.

    d The number of overfilled bottles in a sample of 25 taken from a machine that should overfill 2% of bottles.

> **Hint** The conditions for modelling a situation using a binomial distribution are:
> - a fixed number of trials
> - two possible outcomes
> - a fixed probability of success
> - the trials are independent.

2 The random variable $X \sim B(6, 0.2)$. Find:

   a $P(X = 2)$ **b** $P(X = 4)$ **c** $P(X < 2)$

> **Hint** Use your calculator or the formula
> $P(X = r) = \binom{n}{r} p^r (1 - p)^{n-r}$.

3 The random variable $Y \sim B\left(12, \frac{3}{5}\right)$. Find:

   a $P(Y = 6)$ **b** $P(Y = 10)$ **c** $P(Y \geqslant 9)$

> **Hint** $P(Y \geqslant 9) = P(Y = 9) + P(Y = 10)$
> $+ P(Y = 11) + P(Y = 12)$

(E) 4 Anton spins a fair five-sided spinner 8 times and records the random variable X, the number of times the spinner lands on yellow (Y).

He models this random variable as $X \sim B(n, p)$.

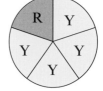

   a State the values of n and p. **(2 marks)**

   b Find:

     i $P(X = 5)$ **ii** $P(X = 3)$ **iii** $P(X \geqslant 7)$ **(3 marks)**

(E/P) 5 Charlotte is testing the lifetime of some batteries. The probability that a battery chosen at random lasts less than 30 hours is 0.12. Charlotte takes a sample of 20 batteries.

   a State any assumptions that are required to model the number of batteries that last less than 30 hours as a binomial distribution. **(2 marks)**

Using this model, find:

   b the probability that exactly 3 batteries last less than 30 hours **(2 marks)**

   c the probability that two or fewer batteries last less than 30 hours. **(3 marks)**

(E/P) 6 In a market research poll, it is found that the probability that a person chosen at random likes chocolate spread is 0.8.

A random sample of 50 people is taken from the poll.

   a State a suitable distribution to model the random variable, X, the number of people in the sample who like chocolate spread. **(1 mark)**

   b Find the probability that:

     i 40 people like chocolate spread

     ii more than 47 people like chocolate spread. **(3 marks)**

(E/P) 7 Dawid rolls a fair six-sided dice 10 times. He records, X, the number of times the dice lands on a prime number.

   a Define a suitable distribution to model X and write down two assumptions that are required for the distribution to be valid. **(2 marks)**

   b Find the probability that Dawid rolls 4 prime numbers. **(2 marks)**

He repeats the experiment 7 times.

   c Find the probability that he rolls 4 prime numbers exactly twice. **(3 marks)**

6.3 Cumulative probabilities

1 The random variable $X \sim B(12, 0.3)$. Find:

   a $P(X \leq 2)$ **b** $P(X < 6)$ **c** $P(X \geq 7)$

> **Hint** Use statistical tables or the binomial cumulative distribution function on your calculator.

2 The random variable $Y \sim B(15, 0.4)$. Find:

   a $P(Y \leq 7)$ **b** $P(Y > 9)$ **c** $P(1 < Y \leq 6)$

> **Hint** $P(1 < Y \leq 6) = P(Y \leq 6) - P(Y \leq 1)$

3 The random variable $T \sim B(35, 0.61)$. Find:

   a $P(T < 25)$ **b** $P(T \geq 28)$ **c** $P(15 \leq T < 30)$

> **Hint** This value of p is not given in the tables so use the binomial cumulative distribution function on your calculator.

(E) 4 The diagram shows a fair spinner.

The spinner is spun 30 times.

Find the probability of it landing on red (R):

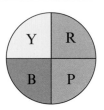

   a fewer than 10 times   **(2 marks)**

   b at least 14 times   **(2 marks)**

   c between 10 and 14 times inclusive.   **(2 marks)**

(E/P) 5 Olivia grows orchids. The probability of a particular plant producing fruit is 0.46. Olivia has many greenhouses, each of which holds 25 plants.

A greenhouse is selected at random. Find the probability that in this greenhouse:

   a there are exactly 8 plants with fruit on them   **(1 mark)**

   b more than 12 plants have fruit on them.   **(2 marks)**

Olivia takes a sample of 6 greenhouses.

   c Find the probability that at least 4 of these greenhouses contain more than 12 plants with fruit on them.   **(3 marks)**

(E/P) 6 Annie is calculating the probability of getting at least 4 sixes when she rolls a fair six-sided dice 25 times.

Her working is shown below.

> Let X be the random variable 'number of sixes'
> $X \sim B\left(25, \frac{1}{6}\right)$
> $P(X > 4) = 1 - P(X \leq 4)$
> $= 1 - 0.5937$
> $= 0.4063$

    a Identify the mistake that Annie has made. **(1 mark)**

    b Calculate the correct probability. **(2 marks)**

E/P **7** Pietro rolls a biased six-sided dice 40 times. The probability of rolling a six is 0.2.

    a State a suitable distribution for the random variable X, the number of sixes that he rolls.

         (1 mark)

    b Find the largest value of k such that $P(X \leq k) < 0.09$. **(2 marks)**

    c Find the smallest value of m such that $P(X > m) < 0.05$. **(2 marks)**

    d Find $P(k \leq X \leq m)$. **(2 marks)**

E/P **8** Frankie is playing a computer game. The probability that she collects the hidden box on each level is 0.4.

    a Given that Frankie plays 15 levels, find the probability that:

       i she collects exactly 8 hidden boxes

       ii more than 10 hidden boxes. **(3 marks)**

    Frankie says the probability that she collects at least 8 boxes is 0.0950.

    b Explain the error that Frankie has made and find the correct probability. **(2 marks)**

Problem solving   Set A

Bronze

A discrete random variable X has probability mass function
$$P(X = x) = \frac{x}{k}, \qquad x = 1, 2, 3, 4$$

    a Find the value of k. **(2 marks)**

    b Show the probability distribution of X in table form. **(2 marks)**

    c Find $P(X > 2)$. **(2 marks)**

Silver

A biased four-sided spinner is numbered from 1 to 4. The probability distribution of the random variable X, the outcome when the spinner is spun, is shown in the table.

x	1	2	3	4
$P(X = x)$	0.2	$2a$	0.35	a

The spinner is spun twice.

Calculate the probability that the total score is:

    a 4 **(3 marks)**

    b greater than 5. **(3 marks)**

Gold

In an experiment a group of cats each repeatedly try to catch a toy mouse.

For each cat, the random variable X represents the number of times the cat catches the mouse in the first five attempts. Karen models X as B(5, 0.2).

a State two assumptions Karen needs to make to use her model. **(2 marks)**

b Using Karen's model, find $P(X \geqslant 3)$. **(1 mark)**

For each cat, the random variable Y represents the number of the attempt on which it first catches the mouse.

c Using Karen's assumptions about this experiment, find $P(Y = 3)$. **(2 marks)**

Ian assumes that in this experiment no cat will need more than 5 attempts to catch the mouse for the first time. He models $P(Y = n)$ as $P(Y = n) = 0.1 + (n - 1)k$

d Find the value of k. **(3 marks)**

e Using Ian's model, find $P(Y = 3)$. **(1 mark)**

f Explain how Karen's and Ian's models differ in describing the probability that a cat catches a mouse in this experiment. **(1 mark)**

Problem solving   Set B

Bronze

A biased coin is tossed 35 times.

a Given that P(heads) = 0.64, write down a suitable distribution for the random variable Y, the number of times the coin lands on heads. **(1 mark)**

b Find the probability that:

   i $P(Y \leqslant 17)$ **ii** $P(5 \leqslant Y \leqslant 20)$ **(3 marks)**

Silver

The random variable $X \sim$ B(30, 0.15). Find:

a the largest value of k such that $P(X < k) < 0.05$ **(1 mark)**

b the smallest number r such that $P(X > r) < 0.01$ **(2 marks)**

c $P(k \leqslant X \leqslant r)$. **(2 marks)**

Gold

A clay pigeon shooter hits a clay with probability 0.65. There are 25 clays in each set. To win a set, the shooter must hit at least 15 clays.

The shooter takes part in 10 sets of 25 clays. Find the probability that the shooter wins:

a exactly 7 of these sets   **(3 marks)**   **b** fewer than 5 of these sets. **(2 marks)**

Now try this → Exam question bank Q2, Q9, Q14, Q16, Q18, Q28, Q33

7.1   Hypothesis testing

1   Alice is testing whether a four-sided dice is biased towards the number three.
She rolls the dice 50 times and counts the number of threes she gets.

    a Describe the test statistic.

    b Write down a suitable null hypothesis.

    c Write down a suitable alternative hypothesis.

> **Hint** The null hypothesis is the hypothesis that you assume to be correct when making your calculations.

2   For each of these hypotheses, state whether they describe a one-tailed or a two-tailed test.

> **Hint** To test whether p is different from a given value you need to use a two-tailed test.

    a $H_0: p = 0.7$, $H_1: p < 0.7$

    b $H_0: p = 0.5$, $H_1: p > 0.5$

    c $H_0: p = 0.4$, $H_1: p \neq 0.4$

E/P 3   A Member of Parliament has found that, from long experience, he gets support from 65% of the adult population of his constituency. A new sample of 50 people is taken and 24 people say that they support him. The Member of Parliament wants to test, at the 5% level of significance, whether or not his support has decreased.

    a Suggest a suitable test statistic. **(1 mark)**

    b Write down two suitable hypotheses. **(2 marks)**

    c Explain the condition under which the null hypothesis is rejected. **(2 marks)**

E/P 4   A cereal manufacturer places a prize in some packets of a type of cereal. The manufacturer claims that there are prizes in 5% of packets. A regular customer purchases 120 packets of the cereal and finds a prize in 15 packets. She wishes to test, at the 10% level of significance, whether the manufacturer is putting prizes in more than 5% of the packets.

    a Write down a suitable test statistic. **(1 mark)**

    b Write down suitable null and alternative hypotheses. **(2 marks)**

    c Explain the condition under which the null hypothesis would be accepted. **(2 marks)**

E/P 5   Georgia runs a car-servicing workshop. She claims that 60% of all services take less than two hours to complete. Gemma, her business partner, thinks that this proportion might be incorrect. She takes a sample of 50 services and finds that five take longer than two hours to complete. She wishes to test, at the 5% significance level, whether Georgia's claim is incorrect.

    a Write down a suitable test statistic. **(1 mark)**

    b Write down suitable null and alternative hypotheses. **(2 marks)**

    c Explain the condition under which the null hypothesis is rejected. **(2 marks)**

7.2   Finding critical values

1   A test statistic has a distribution B(8, p). Given that H$_0$: $p = 0.6$ and H$_1$: $p < 0.6$,

   a find the critical region for the test using a 5% level of significance

   b write down the actual significance level of the test.

2   A test statistic has a distribution B(15, p). Given that H$_0$: $p = 0.3$ and H$_1$: $p > 0.3$,

   a find the critical region for the test using a 10% level of significance

   b write down the actual significance level of the test.

3   A test statistic has distribution B(25, p). Given that H$_0$: $p = 0.42$ and H$_1$: $p \neq 0.42$,

   a find the critical region for the test using a 10% level of significance

   b write down the actual significance level of the test.

(E/P) 4   A florist claims that 20% of hydrangeas will have blue flowers. A regular customer thinks that this proportion is overstated and decides to buy 30 plants in order to test the claim.

   a Describe the test statistic and write down suitable null and alternative hypotheses.   **(3 marks)**

   b Using a 5% level of significance, find the critical region for the customer's test.   **(2 marks)**

   c State the probability of incorrectly rejecting the null hypothesis using this critical region.   **(1 mark)**

(E/P) 5   A hotel typically gets 5-star reviews 60% of the time on a travel website. The hotel owner decides to make some improvements to try and increase this percentage. The owner takes a random sample of 20 reviews after the improvements have taken place.

   a Describe the test statistic and write down suitable null and alternative hypotheses.   **(3 marks)**

   b Using a 10% level of significance, find the critical region for the hotel owner's test.   **(2 marks)**

   c State the actual significance level of the test.   **(1 mark)**

(E/P) 6   A manufacturer of electronic components finds that, over the long term, one component in every 20 of the components produced has a fault. The manufacturer decides to modify the production process and believes that this will change the proportion of components that have a fault.

   a Suggest a suitable model and write down suitable null and alternative hypotheses.   **(3 marks)**

The manufacturer takes a random sample of 50 components.

b Find, at the 20% level of significance, the critical region for a test to check the belief that the proportion of components with a fault has changed. **(4 marks)**

c State the actual significance level of the test. **(1 mark)**

E/P **7** A random variable has distribution B(25, p). A single observation is used to test $H_0: p = 0.3$ against $H_1: p \neq 0.3$.

a Using a 5% level of significance, find the critical region for this test. The probability in each tail should be as close as possible to 0.025. **(3 marks)**

b Write down the actual significance level of the test. **(2 marks)**

7.3 One-tailed tests

1 A single observation, x, is taken from a binomial distribution B(20, p) and a value of 3 is obtained. Use this observation to test $H_0: p = 0.4$ against $H_1: p < 0.4$ using a 2% level of significance.

Hint Assume $X \sim$ B(20, 0.4) and calculate $P(X \leqslant 3)$, and compare this with 0.02.

2 A random variable X has distribution B(25, p). A single observation of $x = 17$ is taken from the distribution. Test, at the 1% level of significance, $H_0: p = 0.45$ against $H_1: p > 0.45$.

Hint You could find $P(X \geqslant 17)$, or you could start by finding the critical region for the test.

E **3** A magician claims to be able to fool a person by sleight of hand 90% of the time. In a sample of n people, X is the number of people who are fooled.

a Write down a suitable distribution to model X. **(1 mark)**

A random sample of 40 people is taken and it is found that 33 are fooled by the sleight of hand. It is believed that the magician's claim of fooling people 90% of the time is overstated.

b Test this claim at the 5% level of significance. State your hypotheses clearly. **(5 marks)**

E/P **4** Tia grows marrows and she finds that over time, 60% of the marrows are longer than 40 cm. Tia uses a new fertiliser. The manufacturer claims the fertiliser will increase the proportion of marrows that are longer than 40 cm.

Tia takes a random sample of 30 marrows and carries out a hypothesis test, at the 5% level of significance, to test the manufacturer's claim.

a Write down Tia's null and alternative hypotheses. **(2 marks)**

b Find the critical region for Tia's test. **(3 marks)**

Tia finds that 25 marrows in her sample are longer than 40 cm.

c Comment on this observation in light of the critical region. **(2 marks)**

E/P 5 Esha makes clay pots. She estimates that 10% of the pots fracture during the firing process in her kiln. She decides to change the type of clay she uses in order to try and reduce the proportion of pots that fracture. She takes a random sample of 50 pots made using the new clay and finds that only one has fractured in the kiln.

Stating your hypotheses clearly and using a 5% level of significance, test whether there is evidence that changing the type of clay has reduced the likelihood of the pots fracturing.

(5 marks)

E/P 6 A random variable has distribution $B(10, p)$. A single observation is taken and a value of 7 obtained.

Briony decides to test $H_0: p = 0.3$ against $H_1: p > 0.3$, using a 1% level of significance.

Her working is shown below.

Let $X \sim B(10, 0.3)$
$P(X = 7) = 0.0090$
Since $0.0090 < 0.01$, reject H_0
There is evidence that $p > 0.3$

Briony has made a mistake in her working.

Explain her mistake and determine the actual result of the test. **(3 marks)**

E/P 7 From experience, a door-to-door carpet salesman knows that the probability that he makes a sale is 0.05. He visits 15 houses in one day.

a Calculate the probability that he makes at least one sale. **(2 marks)**

He decides to change his pitch to try and improve the likelihood of making a sale. On the day after changing his pitch, he visits 26 houses and makes 4 sales.

b Test, at the 5% level of significance, the claim that he has increased his likelihood of making a sale. State your hypotheses clearly. **(5 marks)**

7.4 Two-tailed tests

1 A single observation, x, is taken from a binomial distribution $X \sim B(15, p)$ and a value of 3 is obtained.

Use this observation to test, at the 10% level of significance, $H_0: p = 0.4$ against $H_1: p \neq 0.4$.

Hint Halve the significance level in each tail. You need to work out $P(X \leq 3)$ and compare the answer with 0.05.

2 A random variable has distribution $X \sim B(40, p)$. A single observation of $x = 34$ is taken from the distribution. Test, at the 5% level of significance, $H_0: p = 0.7$ against $H_1: p \neq 0.7$.

Hint Find the probability that X is greater than or equal to 34 given the value of p.

E/P **3** The proportion of people diagnosed with a particular disease nationally is 0.05. A random sample of 200 people is taken from the south west. It is found that 16 people have the disease. Test, at the 5% level of significance, the hypothesis that the proportion of people in the south west who have the disease is different from the national average. State your hypotheses clearly.

(5 marks)

E/P **4** A nutritionist finds that, on average, 10% of her clients are overweight. She decides to introduce a new diet to her clients.

She takes a random sample of 50 clients who have used the new diet.

a Find the critical regions, at the 10% level of significance, to test whether or not the proportion of her clients has changed. **(4 marks)**

b State the actual significance level of the test. **(1 mark)**

From the sample, she finds that 2 clients are overweight.

c Comment on this finding in light of your critical regions. **(2 marks)**

E/P **5** Meghan rolls an eight-sided dice 120 times and finds that it lands on the number eight 25 times.

Use a two-tailed test with a significance level of 5% to determine whether there is sufficient evidence to conclude that the dice is biased. State your hypotheses clearly. **(5 marks)**

E/P **6** A single observation, x, is taken from a binomial distribution B(30, p). This observation is used to test H_0: $p = 0.25$ against H_1: $p \neq 0.25$.

a Using a 10% level of significance, find the critical region for this test. The probability in each tail should be as close as possible to 5%. **(3 marks)**

b State the actual significance level of this test. **(2 marks)**

The actual value of x obtained is 11.

c State a conclusion that can be drawn based on this value, giving a reason for your answer. **(1 mark)**

E/P **7** A chicken farmer knows from experience that one egg in every 50 has a double yolk. The farmer decides to change the type of feed that she uses. She wants to carry out a hypothesis test to determine whether the new feed has affected the chance of a double yolk.

In a random sample of 50 eggs produced by chickens using the new feed, she finds that 3 have double yolks.

Carry out a hypothesis test, at the 10% level of significance, to assess whether the chance of a double yolk has changed. State your hypotheses clearly. **(5 marks)**

Problem solving   Set A

Bronze

A single observation, x, is taken from a binomial distribution $B(30, p)$, and is used to test H_0: $p = 0.36$ against H_1: $p \neq 0.36$.

a Find the critical region for a two-tailed test at the 5% level of significance. **(3 marks)**

b Write down the actual significance level of the test. **(1 mark)**

The value $x = 16$ is observed.

c Comment on this observation in light of your critical region. **(1 mark)**

Silver

A single observation, x, is taken from a binomial distribution $B(35, p)$, and is used to test H_0: $p = 0.45$ against H_1: $p \neq 0.45$.

a Find the critical region for a two-tailed test at the 10% level of significance. The probability in each tail should be as close as possible to 0.05. **(3 marks)**

b Write down the probability of incorrectly rejecting the null hypothesis in this test. **(1 mark)**

The value $x = 22$ is observed.

c Comment on this observation in light of your critical region. **(1 mark)**

Gold

The random variable X is known to have the distribution $B(20, p)$, where p is unknown. Amy uses a single observation from X to test H_0: $p = 0.4$ against H_1: $p \neq 0.4$.

a Find the critical region for Amy's test at the 5% level of significance. **(3 marks)**

Amy decides she will carry out her test 15 times. She will reject H_0 if more than a quarter of her observations lie in the critical region.

b Find the probability that Amy will incorrectly reject H_0. **(3 marks)**

Problem solving   Set B

Bronze

A juggler claims to be able to juggle five balls for over ten minutes 65% of the times she attempts it. A circus owner believes that this proportion is not correct. The juggler attempts to juggle five balls 15 times and juggles for over ten minutes on 13 occasions.

Test, at the 10% level of significance, whether this provides evidence for the circus owner's belief. State your hypotheses clearly. **(5 marks)**

Silver

The outcome of rolling a biased four-sided dice is modelled as a discrete random variable, X, with probability mass function

$$P(X = x) = \frac{x}{k}, \qquad x = 1, 2, 3, 4$$

a Calculate $P(X = 4)$. **(3 marks)**

Doreen claims that the model is incorrect and rolls the dice 50 times. She gets a 4 on 28 occasions.

b Using a 5% level of significance and stating your hypotheses clearly, test Doreen's claim. **(4 marks)**

Gold

A paper company finds that, over time, defects occur at a rate of 1 in every 250 sheets of paper produced. After switching to recycled paper, the company examines a sample of 300 sheets of paper, and finds that it contains 5 defective sheets. An employee decides to carry out a hypothesis test, at the 5% level of significance, to assess the claim that the switch to recycled paper has affected the rate of defects. The employee's working is shown below:

> Let X be the random variable 'number of defects' and $X \sim B(300, p)$
> H_0: $p = 0.004$
> H_1: $p \neq 0.004$
> $P(X \leq 5 \mid p = 0.004) = 0.9985$
> Since $0.9985 > 0.05$, accept H_0
> There is no evidence that the rate of defects has changed.

The employee has made two mistakes.

Explain these mistakes and determine the correct conclusion to the hypothesis test. **(5 marks)**

Now try this → **Exam question bank Q23, Q27, Q29, Q31, Q34**

8 Modelling in mechanics

8.1 Constructing a model

1 The motion of a football after it is kicked by a player can be modelled using the equation $h = 0.6x - 0.06x^2$, where h m is the height of the football above the ground and x m is the horizontal distance travelled.

    a Find the height of the football when it is:

        i struck

        ii at a horizontal distance of 3 m

        iii at a horizontal distance of 6 m.

> **Hint** When the football is struck, $x = 0$.

    b Use the model to predict the height of the football when it is 15 m from the player.

    c Comment on the validity of this prediction.

> **Hint** To answer part **c**, look at the context of the question to determine whether your answer is valid. In this case, h represents the height of the football above the ground so the model is only valid for $h \geqslant 0$.

2 A diver jumps from a diving board into a swimming pool with a depth of 5 m. The height of the diver above the water level, h m, after t seconds can be modelled using the equation $h = -5t^2 + 3t + 8$.

    a Write down the height of the diving board above the water.

    b Find the height of the diver above the water when $t = 1$.

    c Use the model to predict the height of the diver after 3 seconds.

    d Comment on the validity of this prediction.

3 When Rashid takes a throw in the shot put, the motion of the shot can be modelled using the equation $h = 0.8x - 0.05x^2$, where h m is the height of the shot above Rashid's chest (the point from which it's thrown) and x m is the horizontal distance travelled.

    a Find the height of the shot above Rashid's chest when:

        i $x = 2$ **ii** $x = 5$ **iii** $x = 10$

    b Use the model to predict the height of the shot above Rashid's chest when $x = 20$. Comment on the validity of this prediction.

Ⓟ 4 A car decelerates from 60 mph to 20 mph in 8 seconds. A quadratic equation of the form $d = 26.8t - kt^2$ can be used to model the distance travelled by the car, where d metres is the distance travelled in time t seconds.

    a Given that when $t = 2$ the distance travelled by the car is 49.1 m, use the model to find the distance travelled when the car reaches 20 mph.

> **Hint** Substitute the values given in the question into the model and solve the corresponding equation to find k.

    b Write down the range of values of t for which the model is valid.

5 The model for the motion of a football given in question **1** is only valid when h is positive.

Find the range of values of x for which the model is valid.

6 The model for the height of the diver above the water given in question **2** is only valid from the time the diver dives until the time the diver enters the water. Find the range of values of t for which the model is valid.

7 The model for the motion of Rashid's shot given in question **3** is only valid when h is positive.

a Find the range of values of x for which the model is valid.

b Work out the maximum height of Rashid's shot above his chest.

When Sam takes a throw in the shot put, the motion of the shot can be modelled using the equation $h = 0.6x - 0.04x^2$, where h m is the height of the shot above his chest and x m is the horizontal distance travelled. The player that throws the shot furthest wins the competition.

c Use the models given to determine who will win the contest, and find the distance by which they win. Assume the shot finishes at the same height as it started in each case.

P **8** The motion of a netball as it leaves a player's hand and passes through the net is modelled using the equation $h = 1.8 + 1.2x - 0.2x^2$, where h m is the height of the netball above the ground and x m is the horizontal distance travelled.

a Write down the height of the ball when it leaves the player's hand. **(1 mark)**

b Find the two values of x for which the netball is exactly 3.4 m above the ground. **(2 marks)**

The model is only valid for $0 \leqslant x \leqslant k$, where k m is the horizontal distance of the net from the player. Given that the height of the net is 2.8 m and that the netball passes through the net as it is travelling downwards:

c find the range of values of x for which the model is valid **(1 mark)**

d work out the maximum height of the netball. **(2 marks)**

8.2 Modelling assumptions

1 Two children of different masses are sitting on a see-saw that rests on a support.

State the effect on any calculations made using this model based on the following assumptions:

a the children are modelled as particles

b the see-saw is modelled as a uniform rod

c the support is modelled as a smooth peg

d air resistance is negligible

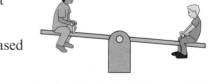

Hint Modelling assumptions simplify a problem. For example, by modelling a child as a particle you assume that the child's weight acts at a single point.

2 A mechanical engineer constructs a mathematical model to predict the behaviour of a car on a particular racetrack. The engineer models the racetrack as smooth.

a Describe the effects of this modelling assumption.

b Comment on its validity in this situation.

> **Hint** Modelling assumptions can affect the validity of a model. Think about whether modelling the racetrack as smooth is a reasonable assumption.

3 A bungee jumper wants to model her descent. She models the bungee cord as an inextensible string. Explain why this modelling assumption is unlikely to be suitable for this situation.

4 Make a list of the assumptions you might make to model a car and trailer connected by a tow-bar.

(P) 5 A small stone is dropped from a height and falls vertically to the ground.

a Make a list of the assumptions you might make to create a simple model.

b A feather is dropped from the same height as the stone. Describe the differences between the motion of the stone and the motion of the feather:

i using the same model for the feather and the stone

ii in real life.

c With reference to your answer to part **b**, suggest a possible refinement to your model.

8.3 Quantities and units

1 Convert to base SI units:

a $45\,\text{km}\,\text{h}^{-1}$

b $1800\,\text{g}$ per minute

c $7\,\text{g}\,\text{cm}^{-3}$

d $540\,\text{g}\,\text{m}^{-3}$

e $1.2 \times 10^{-4}\,\text{kg}\,\text{cm}^{-3}$

f $4.1 \times 10^{5}\,\text{g}\,\text{cm}^{-3}$

> **Hint** Kilograms (kg), metres (m) and seconds (s) are all base SI units.

2 Write down the names of the forces shown in each of these diagrams.

a A parachute jumper descending to the ground after opening the parachute.

b A car driving along a level road.

c An inflatable dinghy being towed along a lake by a boat.

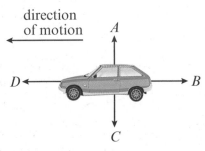

direction of motion

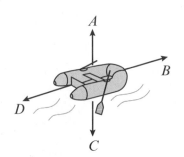

8.4 Working with vectors

1 Julia drives from her home along a straight road to work at a constant speed of 42 mph.

On her way home from work she stops at her daughter's school to pick her up.

She drives from work to the school at a constant speed of 28 mph.

She drives from the school to her home at a constant speed of 34 mph.

Julia's home, work and the school all lie on a straight line, as shown in the diagram.

Taking the positive direction as shown in the diagram, state Julia's:

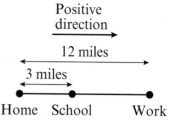

a velocity on the journey from her home to work

b displacement from her home when she reaches work

c velocity on the journey from work to the school

d displacement from work when she reaches the school

e velocity on the journey from the school to her home.

> **Hint** You need to choose a positive direction when considering motion in a straight line. When an object is moving in the opposite direction to the positive direction its velocity is negative.

2 Match each scenario **i–iv** with the motion of each object **a–d**.

	ⓐ	ⓑ	ⓒ	ⓓ	Positive direction
Velocity	+ve	+ve	−ve	−ve	
Acceleration	+ve	−ve	−ve	+ve	

i A ball falls to the ground and its speed increases.

ii A ball is thrown upwards and its speed decreases.

iii A rocket is launched upwards and its speed increases.

iv A helicopter lowers to the ground and its speed decreases.

> **Hint** When the sign of the acceleration and the sign of the velocity are different, the acceleration is opposing the direction of motion, so the particle is slowing down.

3 The velocity of a particle is given by $\mathbf{v} = 8\mathbf{i} + 12\mathbf{j}\,\mathrm{m\,s^{-1}}$. Find:

a the speed of the particle

b the angle the direction of motion of the particle makes with the unit vector **i**.

> **Hint** Draw a diagram. The speed of the particle is the magnitude of the vector **v**. You can use trigonometry to find the direction of **v**.

4 The acceleration of a car is given by $\mathbf{a} = -7\mathbf{i} + 5\mathbf{j}\,\mathrm{m\,s^{-2}}$. Find:

a the magnitude of the acceleration of the car

b the angle the direction of the acceleration vector of the car makes with the unit vector **j**.

E/P **5** A car drives from A to B and then from B to C.

The displacement from A to B is $10\mathbf{i} + 5\mathbf{j}$ km.

The displacement from B to C is $16\mathbf{i} - 13\mathbf{j}$ km.

a Find the magnitude of the displacement from A to C. **(3 marks)**

b Find the angle $\overrightarrow{AC}$ makes with the unit vector $\mathbf{i}$. **(2 marks)**

E/P **6** A man jogs in a straight line from P to Q and then in a straight line from Q to R.

The displacement from P to Q is $240\mathbf{i} - 600\mathbf{j}$ m.

The displacement from Q to R is $450\mathbf{i} + 350\mathbf{j}$ m.

a Find the magnitude of the displacement from P to R. **(3 marks)**

b Find the total distance, correct to the nearest metre, that the man has jogged in getting from P to R. **(3 marks)**

c Find the angle that $\overrightarrow{PR}$ makes with the unit vector $\mathbf{j}$. **(2 marks)**

Problem solving Set A

Bronze

The motion of a ball can be modelled using the equation $h = 1.4 + 0.5x - 0.1x^2$, where h m is the height of the ball above the ground and x m is the horizontal distance travelled.

a Find the height of the ball when:

i $x = 2$ **ii** $x = 4$ **iii** $x = 6$ **(3 marks)**

b Use the model to predict the height of the ball when $x = 10$.
Comment on the validity of this prediction. **(2 marks)**

Silver

The motion of a volleyball after it is served by a player is modelled using the equation $h = 1.2 + x - 0.2x^2$, where h m is the height of the volleyball above the ground and x m is the horizontal distance travelled.

a Write down the height of the ball when it leaves the player's hand. **(1 mark)**

The model for the motion of a volleyball is only valid when h is positive.

b Find the range of values of x for which the model is valid. **(2 marks)**

c A player stands k m from the net when the volleyball is served. The volleyball net is 2 m high. Given that the volleyball clears the net, find the range of possible values of k. **(3 marks)**

d Find the maximum height of the volleyball according to this model. **(2 marks)**

Gold

A golf ball is struck from the top of a vertical cliff 25 m above water level. It enters the water at a horizontal distance of 60 m from the cliff face.

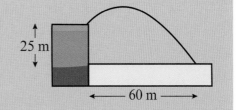

The motion of the golf ball is modelled by the equation $h = px - 0.02x^2 + q$, $0 \leqslant x \leqslant 60$, where h m is the height of the golf ball above the water, x m is the horizontal distance from the cliff face, and p and q are constants.

Find the maximum height of the golf ball above the water. **(4 marks)**

Problem solving Set B

In these questions, the unit vector **j** is directed due north and the unit vector **i** is directed due east.

Bronze

The velocity of a particle is given by $\mathbf{v} = 5\mathbf{i} + 6\mathbf{j}\,\mathrm{m\,s^{-1}}$. Find:

a the speed of the particle **(2 marks)**

b the angle the direction of motion of the particle makes with the unit vector **i**. **(2 marks)**

Silver

An aeroplane flies from airport A to make three deliveries at airports B, C and D, in that order.

The displacement from A to B is $120\mathbf{i} - 200\mathbf{j}\,\mathrm{km}$.

The displacement from B to C is $150\mathbf{i} + 180\mathbf{j}\,\mathrm{km}$.

The displacement from C to D is $-250\mathbf{i} + 80\mathbf{j}\,\mathrm{km}$.

The aeroplane has enough fuel to fly 800 km, and flies in a straight line between each airport.

a Does the aeroplane have enough fuel make the three deliveries and return to airport A? Explain your answer fully. **(4 marks)**

b Find the bearing from D to A. Give your answer as a three-figure bearing. **(3 marks)**

Gold

A hiker walks in a straight line from P to Q and then in a straight line from Q to R.

The displacement from P to Q is $900\mathbf{i} - 400\mathbf{j}\,\mathrm{m}$.

The displacement from Q to R is $-500\mathbf{i} + a\mathbf{j}\,\mathrm{m}$.

The magnitude of the displacement from P to R is 412.3 m.

The total distance the hiker travels from P to R is 1568 m.

Find the value of a to the nearest metre, showing your working clearly. **(6 marks)**

9 Constant acceleration

9.1 Displacement–time graphs

1 This is a displacement–time graph for a car travelling along a straight road. The journey is divided into three stages labelled A, B and C.

a Work out the velocity of the car for each of the three stages of the journey, in $km\,h^{-1}$.

> **Hint** To find the velocity in $km\,h^{-1}$, convert the time from minutes to hours.

b State the average velocity for the whole journey.

c Work out the average speed for the whole journey.

> **Hint** To find the average speed, divide the total distance travelled by the total time taken.

(P) 2 This is a displacement–time graph for a train journey between Town A and Town C. The journey includes a stop to change trains at Town B. The three towns lie on a straight line.

During the first part of the journey, a third of the total distance, d, is covered in two hours. After a one-hour stop, the remaining distance is covered in five hours.

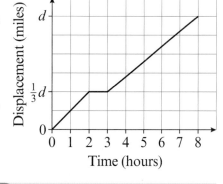

Given that the average velocity of the train between Town A and Town B is 65 mph, find:

a the total distance of the journey, d

> **Hint** To answer part **a**, remember that the gradient represents the velocity, so set up an equation and solve for d.

b the average velocity of the train between Town B and Town C

c the average velocity for the whole journey (including the stop).

(P) 3 Ken leaves home and cycles north in a straight line. He then travels back along the same route, continuing past his home. Later, he returns to his home.

The diagram shows a displacement–time graph for his journey divided into five stages, A–E.

a Work out the velocity for each stage of the journey.

b Using the graph, find the length of time between Ken setting off, and passing his home again.

c Using the graph, find the total length of time that Ken is more than 20 km from home.

d Calculate the average speed for his entire journey.

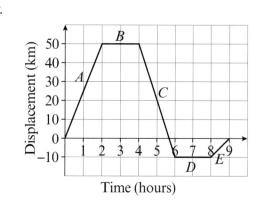

4 Rushanara jumps from a diving board into a swimming pool. Rushanara is modelled as travelling in a straight vertical line. The displacement–time graph shows her vertical motion above the pool.

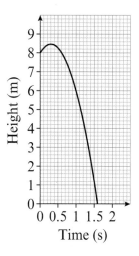

a State the height of the diving board.

b Using the graph, estimate Rushanara's maximum height above the pool and the time at which she reaches that height.

c Write down Rushanara's velocity when she reaches the highest point.

d Describe the motion of Rushanara:

   i from the time she jumps until she reaches her highest point

   ii after reaching the highest point.

9.2 Velocity–time graphs

1 The diagram shows a velocity–time graph illustrating the motion of a runner moving along a straight road for a period of 60 seconds.

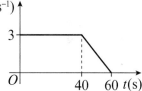

For the first 40 seconds, the runner moves at a constant speed of $3\,\mathrm{m\,s^{-1}}$. The runner then decelerates at a constant rate, stopping after a further 20 seconds.

a Find the displacement of the runner from the starting point after this 60-second period.

b Work out the rate at which the runner decelerates.

> **Hint** For part **b**, the gradient represents the acceleration.

2 A car accelerates uniformly from rest at point A to a velocity of $18\,\mathrm{m\,s^{-1}}$ in 8 seconds.

This velocity is then maintained for a further 12 seconds until the car passes point B.

a Sketch a velocity–time graph to illustrate the motion of the car.

b Find the rate at which the car accelerates.

c Find the distance from A to B.

> **Hint** For part **c**, the area between a velocity–time graph and the horizontal axis represents the distance travelled.

3 A cyclist is moving along a straight road. The cyclist starts from rest at point A and accelerates uniformly at a constant rate of $0.6\,\mathrm{m\,s^{-2}}$ for 20 seconds until reaching point B. The cyclist maintains a constant velocity for 30 seconds until reaching point C. The cyclist then decelerates uniformly for 10 seconds, coming to rest at point D.

a Sketch a velocity–time graph to illustrate the motion of the cyclist.

b Find the deceleration of the cyclist during the journey from C to D.

c Find the distance from A to D.

d Find the cyclist's displacement from the starting point after 30 seconds.

E/P 4 A particle moves along a straight line. The particle accelerates uniformly from rest to a velocity of $10\,\mathrm{m\,s^{-1}}$ in T seconds. The particle then travels at a constant velocity of $10\,\mathrm{m\,s^{-1}}$ for 50 seconds. The particle then decelerates uniformly to rest in a further $3T$ seconds.

 a Sketch a velocity–time graph to illustrate the motion of the particle. **(3 marks)**

 Given that the total displacement of the particle is $1000\,\mathrm{m}$,

 b find the value of T. **(3 marks)**

E/P 5 A particle is travelling in a straight line with velocity $u\,\mathrm{m\,s^{-1}}$. At point A the particle accelerates at a constant rate, reaching a velocity of $25\,\mathrm{m\,s^{-1}}$ after 10 seconds. The particle then immediately decelerates at a constant rate, coming to rest at point B after another 10 seconds.

 a Sketch a velocity–time graph to illustrate the motion. **(3 marks)**

 Given that the distance between A and B is $325\,\mathrm{m}$,

 b find the value of u. **(3 marks)**

E/P 6 Nishant runs a $100\,\mathrm{m}$ race in a straight line. He starts from rest and accelerates uniformly for 1 second, reaching a speed of $10\,\mathrm{m\,s^{-1}}$. He maintains this speed for 5 seconds and then accelerates uniformly for 4 seconds, reaching a top speed of $k\,\mathrm{m\,s^{-1}}$.

 a Sketch a velocity–time graph to illustrate the motion. **(3 marks)**

 Nishant runs $100\,\mathrm{m}$ in 10 seconds.

 b Find the value of k. **(3 marks)**

 c Work out the acceleration of Nishant during the last 4 seconds of the race. **(2 marks)**

 d Suggest one improvement that could be made to the model of the motion of the sprinter during the race in order to make the model more realistic. **(1 mark)**

9.3 Constant acceleration formulae 1

1 A particle is moving in a straight line with constant acceleration $5\,\mathrm{m\,s^{-2}}$. Initially, the velocity of the particle is $3\,\mathrm{m\,s^{-1}}$. Find the velocity of the particle after 10 seconds.

> **Hint** You need v and you know u, a and t so you can use $v = u + at$.

2 A cyclist decelerates uniformly while travelling on a straight road. The cyclist is initially travelling with velocity $9\,\mathrm{m\,s^{-1}}$ and comes to rest in 20 seconds. Find the deceleration of the cyclist.

> **Hint** For each question, write down the values you know and the values you need to find. This will help you to decide which formula to use.

3 A particle is moving in a straight line with constant acceleration. At time $t = 0$, the velocity of the particle is $1.2\,\mathrm{m\,s^{-1}}$. At time $t = 7$, the velocity of the particle is $6.8\,\mathrm{m\,s^{-1}}$. Find the distance travelled in these 7 seconds.

> **Hint** You need s and you know u, v and t, so use $s = \left(\dfrac{u + v}{2}\right)t$.

4   A car decelerates uniformly while travelling on a straight road. The car passes two signposts that are 720 m apart. The car passes the first signpost with velocity $26\,\text{m s}^{-1}$, and the second signpost with velocity $10\,\text{m s}^{-1}$. Find the time taken to travel between the two signposts.

5   A car decelerates uniformly at a rate of $2.4\,\text{m s}^{-2}$ while travelling on a straight road. The car passes two signposts, taking 8 seconds to travel between them. As it passes the second signpost, the car has velocity $1.8\,\text{m s}^{-1}$. Find the velocity of the car as it passes the first signpost.

6   A particle moves in a straight line from a point A to a point B with constant acceleration. The particle takes 15 seconds to travel 120 m from A to B. The velocity of the particle at point A is $4.5\,\text{m s}^{-1}$. Find the velocity of the particle at point B.

7   A particle is moving in a straight line with constant acceleration $4\,\text{m s}^{-2}$. The velocity of the particle at A is $4\,\text{m s}^{-1}$ and the velocity of the particle at B is $14\,\text{m s}^{-1}$. Find:

   a   the time taken for the particle to move from A to B

   b   the distance from A to B.

8   A particle moves in a straight line with constant acceleration from point A to point B. The particle takes 25 seconds to travel 400 m from A to B. The velocity of the particle at point B is $18\,\text{m s}^{-1}$. Find:

   a   the velocity of the particle at point A b   the acceleration of the particle.

9   A car accelerates uniformly while travelling on a straight road. The car is initially at rest and reaches a velocity of $15\,\text{m s}^{-1}$ in 30 seconds. Find:

   a   the acceleration of the car

   b   the distance the car has travelled after 30 seconds

   c   the velocity after 20 seconds

   d   the distance the car has travelled after 20 seconds.

10   A car travels 560 m in a straight line between points A and B. The velocity of the car at point A is $68.4\,\text{km h}^{-1}$ and the velocity of the car at point B is $32.4\,\text{km h}^{-1}$. Find:

   a   the time taken to travel from A to B

   b   the deceleration of the car.

11   Alex and Ben are cyclists racing on a straight 1 km road.

   Alex accelerates uniformly from rest to a velocity of $8\,\text{m s}^{-1}$ in 20 seconds. He then maintains the velocity of $8\,\text{m s}^{-1}$ for the rest of race.

   Ben accelerates uniformly from rest to a velocity of $9\,\text{m s}^{-1}$ in 50 seconds. He then maintains the velocity of $9\,\text{m s}^{-1}$ for the rest of race.

   Both cyclists start at the same time. Determine who wins the race.

(E/P) **12** A particle is moving in a straight line with constant deceleration between points A and B. The velocity of the particle at A is $22\,\text{m}\,\text{s}^{-1}$. The particle travels the $57\,\text{m}$ from A to B in 3 seconds.

    a Show that the deceleration of the particle is $2\,\text{m}\,\text{s}^{-2}$.   **(4 marks)**

    After reaching B, the particle continues to move along the same straight line with the same constant deceleration. It comes to rest at point C.

    b Find the distance AC.   **(4 marks)**

(E/P) **13** A particle is moving in a straight line with constant acceleration $a\,\text{m}\,\text{s}^{-2}$.

    The particle travels through points A, B and C at times $t = 0$, 5 and 15 seconds respectively.

    The particle has velocity $15\,\text{m}\,\text{s}^{-1}$ at point B and velocity $29\,\text{m}\,\text{s}^{-1}$ at point C.

    a Show that the velocity of the particle at point A is $8\,\text{m}\,\text{s}^{-1}$ and find the value of a.   **(4 marks)**

    b Find the ratio of the distances $AB : BC$.   **(3 marks)**

9.4   Constant acceleration formulae 2

1 A particle is moving in a straight line with constant acceleration $3\,\text{m}\,\text{s}^{-2}$. It passes a point A with velocity $4\,\text{m}\,\text{s}^{-1}$ and later passes through a point B, where $AB = 100\,\text{m}$. Find the velocity of the particle as it passes through B.

> **Hint** You need v and you know u, a and s so you can use $v^2 = u^2 + 2as$.

2 A cyclist accelerates at a constant rate along a straight horizontal road. She starts from rest and reaches a velocity of $16\,\text{m}\,\text{s}^{-1}$ after travelling $80\,\text{m}$. Find her acceleration.

> **Hint** Use $v^2 = u^2 + 2as$. Substitute the values of u, v and s and then solve the equation to find a.

3 A particle is moving in a straight line with constant acceleration $2.4\,\text{m}\,\text{s}^{-2}$. The particle's velocity is $2\,\text{m}\,\text{s}^{-1}$ as it passes a point A, and 10 seconds later it passes a point B. Find the distance AB.

> **Hint** You need s and you know u, t and a, so use $s = ut + \frac{1}{2}at^2$. Always write down the formula you are using before you substitute any values.

4 A particle P is moving on the x-axis with constant deceleration. At time $t = 0$, the particle P passes through the origin O and is moving in the positive x-direction with speed $16\,\text{m}\,\text{s}^{-1}$. When $t = 8$, P is $32\,\text{m}$ from O. Find the magnitude of the deceleration.

5 A car is decelerating at a constant rate of $1.5\,\text{m}\,\text{s}^{-2}$ along a straight horizontal road between points A and B. The distance between points A and B is $75\,\text{m}$ and the car has velocity $8\,\text{m}\,\text{s}^{-1}$ when it passes point B. Find the velocity of the car at A.

6 A car is moving along a straight road with uniform acceleration $3.5\,\text{m}\,\text{s}^{-2}$. The car travels through a junction at speed $6\,\text{m}\,\text{s}^{-1}$. A second junction is $160\,\text{m}$ further down the road. Find the time taken for the car to travel between the two junctions.

7 A car approaches a stop sign at a constant speed of $12.5\,\text{m}\,\text{s}^{-1}$. When the car is $50\,\text{m}$ from the stop sign, the driver applies the brakes with a force that causes the car to decelerate at a constant rate of $1.5\,\text{m}\,\text{s}^{-2}$. Determine whether or not the car will stop before the stop sign.

8 A train is moving along a straight horizontal track with constant deceleration $0.25\,\text{m}\,\text{s}^{-2}$. The train passes a signal when travelling with velocity $54\,\text{km}\,\text{h}^{-1}$, and then passes a second signal at a velocity of $36\,\text{km}\,\text{h}^{-1}$. Find the distance between the signals.

9 A car accelerates from rest to $30\,\text{m}\,\text{s}^{-1}$ over a distance of $500\,\text{m}$.

Kieran models the car as travelling in a straight line with uniform acceleration.

a Use this model to find the velocity of the car after it has travelled a distance of $200\,\text{m}$.

(4 marks)

In fact, after it has travelled $200\,\text{m}$, the velocity of the car is found to be $16\,\text{m}\,\text{s}^{-1}$.

b Comment on Kieran's model, and describe the acceleration of the car in light of this information. **(1 mark)**

10 A particle moves along a straight line, from a point P to a point Q, with constant deceleration. The distance from P to Q is $450\,\text{m}$. The particle takes 20 seconds to move from P to Q and the speed of the particle at Q is $18\,\text{m}\,\text{s}^{-1}$. Find:

a the deceleration of the particle **(2 marks)**

b the speed of the particle at P. **(2 marks)**

11 A particle moves along a straight line with constant acceleration $1.1\,\text{m}\,\text{s}^{-2}$. The particle moves $250\,\text{m}$ in 19 seconds. Find to 1 decimal place:

a the initial velocity of the particle **(2 marks)**

b the final velocity of the particle. **(2 marks)**

12 A motorcycle accelerates at a constant rate of $0.16\,\text{m}\,\text{s}^{-2}$ along a straight horizontal road between points A and B which are $400\,\text{m}$ apart. The motorcycle has velocity $18\,\text{m}\,\text{s}^{-1}$ when it passes point B. Find the time taken to travel from A to B. **(4 marks)**

13 A particle accelerates uniformly from point A to point B in 20 seconds. The velocities at A and B are $3\,\text{m}\,\text{s}^{-1}$ and $28\,\text{m}\,\text{s}^{-1}$ respectively. Given that M is the midpoint of AB, find the length of time it takes for the particle to travel from A to M. **(6 marks)**

14 A particle moves along a straight line, with constant deceleration. It passes the points A, B and C at times $t = 0$, 4 and 10 respectively. Given that AB is $55.2\,\text{m}$ and AC is $120\,\text{m}$:

a find the initial velocity of the particle **(5 marks)**

b find the time when the particle comes to rest. **(4 marks)**

9.5 Vertical motion under gravity

1 A ball is dropped from a point 8 m above the ground with initial velocity $0\,\text{m}\,\text{s}^{-1}$. Find:

  a the speed of the ball after 1 second

  b the distance the ball has fallen after 1 second

  c the speed of the ball when it hits the ground

  d the time taken for the ball to hit the ground.

> **Hint** An object moving vertically under gravity can be modelled as a particle with a constant downward acceleration of $g = 9.8\,\text{m}\,\text{s}^{-2}$.

2 A particle is thrown vertically downward from the top of a tower with speed $12\,\text{m}\,\text{s}^{-1}$. It reaches the ground in 2 seconds. Find:

  a the height of the tower

  b the speed of the particle when it hits the ground.

> **Hint** As the particle is moving downwards throughout its motion, it is sensible to take the downwards direction as positive.

3 A particle is thrown vertically downwards from the top of an 18 m tower. The particle hits the ground after 1 second. Find:

  a the speed at which the particle was thrown from the tower

  b the speed of the particle when it hits the ground.

4 A ball is projected vertically upwards with speed $36\,\text{m}\,\text{s}^{-1}$ from a point on the ground. Find:

  a the velocity of the ball after 3 seconds

  b the time of flight of the ball.

> **Hint** The time of flight is the total time that the ball is in motion; from the time that it is projected to the time that it stops moving. Here the ball will stop when it hits the ground, i.e. when $s = 0$.

5 A ball is projected vertically upwards with speed $11\,\text{m}\,\text{s}^{-1}$ from a point on the ground. Find:

  a the greatest height above the point of projection reached by the ball

  b the time taken to reach this height.

6 A particle is thrown vertically upwards with speed $u\,\text{m}\,\text{s}^{-1}$ from the ground. The particle reaches a maximum height of 10 m during its flight. Find:

  a the speed at which the particle was thrown   **b** the time of flight of the particle.

(E/P) 7 Isabel makes a dive from a high springboard into a diving pool. She leaves the springboard with speed $7\,\text{m}\,\text{s}^{-1}$ upwards. When she leaves the springboard, she is 5 m above the surface of the pool. Isabel is modelled as a particle moving vertically under gravity alone and it is assumed that she does not hit the springboard as she descends.

  a Find the time taken for Isabel to reach the surface of the pool. **(3 marks)**

  b Find her speed when she reaches the surface of the pool. **(3 marks)**

In a refined model, the effect of air resistance is included. This refined model is now used to find the time taken by Isabel to reach the surface of the pool.

  c How would this new value of the time taken for Isabel to reach the surface of the pool compare with the value found using the initial model in part **a**? **(1 mark)**

P 8 A particle is projected upwards from a point which is x m above the ground with speed $4.5\,\mathrm{m\,s^{-1}}$. The time of flight for the particle is 2 seconds. Find the value of x. **(4 marks)**

P 9 A particle is projected vertically upwards with speed $15\,\mathrm{m\,s^{-1}}$. Find the total time for which the particle is 10 m or more above its point of projection. **(4 marks)**

P 10 Pebble A is dropped from a tower 25 m high with initial velocity $0\,\mathrm{m\,s^{-1}}$. One second later, pebble B is thrown downwards from the same tower with initial velocity $u\,\mathrm{m\,s^{-1}}$. The two pebbles hit the ground at exactly the same time. Find the value of u to 3 significant figures. **(5 marks)**

P 11 A ball is thrown vertically upwards from a point which is 10 m above the ground with speed $u\,\mathrm{m\,s^{-1}}$. The ball hits the ground with speed $2u\,\mathrm{m\,s^{-1}}$. Find:

a the value of u **(5 marks)**

b the time of flight of the ball. **(3 marks)**

P 12 A stone A falls vertically from rest from the top of a tower 90 m high. At the same time as A begins to fall, another stone B is projected vertically upwards from the bottom of the tower with speed $36\,\mathrm{m\,s^{-1}}$. The stones collide. Find the time elapsed until the collision. **(5 marks)**

Problem solving — Set A

Bronze

A sprinter runs a straight 200 m race in T seconds. In a model of this race, it is assumed that, starting from rest, the sprinter accelerates uniformly for 6 seconds and reaches a speed of $6.6\,\mathrm{m\,s^{-1}}$. The sprinter maintains this speed for the rest of the race.

a Sketch a velocity–time graph for the motion of the sprinter during the whole race. **(2 marks)**

b Find the acceleration of the sprinter during the first 6 seconds of the race. **(1 mark)**

c Find the distance run by the sprinter in the first 6 seconds of the race. **(1 mark)**

d Find the value of T to 3 significant figures. **(3 marks)**

Silver

Two particles A and B are moving in the same direction along the same straight horizontal road. At $t = 0$, A is at point O and is moving with velocity $20\,\mathrm{m\,s^{-1}}$. A decelerates uniformly, and comes to rest at point X which is 400 m from O. At time $t = 0$, B is at point O and moves with constant velocity $12\,\mathrm{m\,s^{-1}}$. From $t = T$ seconds, B decelerates uniformly and comes to rest at the same point X at the same instant as A does.

a Sketch, on the same set of axes, the velocity–time graphs of the two particles for the period from $t = 0$ to the time when they both come to rest at the point X. **(3 marks)**

b Find the value of T. **(4 marks)**

Gold

Two particles P and Q are moving in the same direction along the same straight horizontal road. At $t = 0$, P is at point O and is moving with constant velocity $8\,\text{m s}^{-1}$. From $t = T$ seconds, P decelerates uniformly, coming to rest at point X which is $450\,\text{m}$ from O.

At time $t = 10$, Q is at point O. It is moving with velocity $10\,\text{m s}^{-1}$ and decelerating uniformly. Q comes to rest at point X at the same instant as P.

a By sketching the velocity–time graphs of the two particles, or otherwise, find the value of T.

(4 marks)

b Find the deceleration of each particle and show that the two particles never have the same instantaneous velocity before they come to rest. (5 marks)

Problem solving Set B

Bronze

A ball is projected vertically upwards from a point which is $x\,\text{m}$ above the ground. The ball has speed $25\,\text{m s}^{-1}$ when it hits the ground. The time of flight of the ball is 4.5 seconds.

Find:

a the speed at which the ball was projected (2 marks)

b the value of x. (3 marks)

Silver

A ball is projected vertically upwards from a point that is $6\,\text{m}$ above the ground. The ball reaches a maximum height of $13\,\text{m}$ above the ground during its flight, before coming to rest on the ground. Find the total time of flight of the ball. (4 marks)

Gold

A particle is projected vertically upwards with a speed of $24.5\,\text{m s}^{-1}$ from a point A.

The point B is h metres above A. The particle moves freely under gravity and is above B for 2 seconds. Calculate the value of h. (5 marks)

Now try this → **Exam question bank Q37, Q39, Q40, Q42, Q43, Q45, Q48, Q51, Q52, Q55**

10.1 Force diagrams

1 A crate is suspended motionless from a rope. Draw a force diagram to show all the forces acting on the crate.

2 A particle of weight 12 N sits at rest on a horizontal plane. State the value of the normal reaction acting on the particle.

3 Given that each of the particles is stationary, work out the values of P and Q:

> **Hint** When a particle is stationary, the forces are all balanced.

a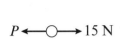

b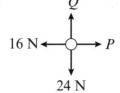

c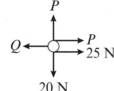

4 Each diagram shows a particle at rest acted on by a set of forces. The particle is at rest in each case. In each case, find the values of p and q.

a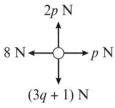

b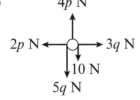

c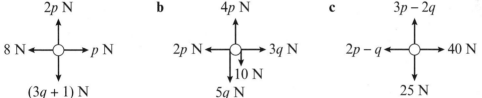

5 Each diagram shows the forces acting on a particle.

  i Work out the size and direction of the resultant force.

  ii Describe the motion of the particle.

a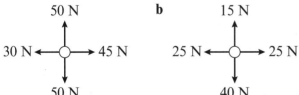

b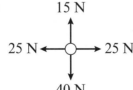

6 A car with weight 20 000 N is moving along a horizontal level road. The car's engine provides a forward thrust of 6000 N. The total resistance is modelled as a constant force of magnitude 800 N.

  a By modelling the car as a particle, draw a force diagram to show the forces acting on the car.

  b Calculate the resultant force acting on the car.

7 A lorry is moving along a horizontal level road. The lorry's engine provides a constant driving force. The motion of the lorry is opposed by a constant resistance.

  a Modelling the lorry as a particle, draw a force diagram to show the forces acting on the lorry.

  b Given that the resultant force acting on the lorry is 7500 N in the direction of motion, and that the magnitude of the driving force is three times the magnitude of the resistance force, calculate the magnitude of the resistance.

10.2 Forces as vectors

1 In each part of the question a particle is acted upon by the forces given. Work out the resultant force acting on the particle.

> **Hint** You can find the resultant force by adding the vectors.

a $(2\mathbf{i} - 4\mathbf{j})\,\text{N}$ and $(-\mathbf{i} + 5\mathbf{j})\,\text{N}$

b $\begin{pmatrix}4\\6\end{pmatrix}\text{N}$ and $\begin{pmatrix}-2\\-5\end{pmatrix}\text{N}$

c $(\mathbf{i} - 2\mathbf{j})\,\text{N}$, $(4\mathbf{i} - 2\mathbf{j})\,\text{N}$ and $(-2\mathbf{i} + 6\mathbf{j})\,\text{N}$

d $\begin{pmatrix}-2\\5\end{pmatrix}\text{N}$, $\begin{pmatrix}0\\7\end{pmatrix}\text{N}$ and $\begin{pmatrix}3\\-8\end{pmatrix}\text{N}$

2 The forces $\begin{pmatrix}3\\4\end{pmatrix}\text{N}$, $\begin{pmatrix}2\\-3\end{pmatrix}\text{N}$ and $\begin{pmatrix}a\\b\end{pmatrix}\text{N}$ act on an object which is in equilibrium. Find the values of a and b.

> **Hint** If an object is in equilibrium, then the resultant force is zero.

3 The forces $\begin{pmatrix}-2\\3\end{pmatrix}\text{N}$, $\begin{pmatrix}5\\-6\end{pmatrix}\text{N}$, $\begin{pmatrix}-6\\4\end{pmatrix}\text{N}$ and $\begin{pmatrix}a\\b\end{pmatrix}\text{N}$ act on an object which is in equilibrium. Find the values of a and b.

4 The forces $(a\mathbf{i} + b\mathbf{j})\,\text{N}$, $(8\mathbf{i} + 2b\mathbf{j})\,\text{N}$ and $(-3a\mathbf{i} - 8\mathbf{j})\,\text{N}$ act on an object which is in equilibrium. Find the values of a and b.

5 For each of the following forces find:
   i the magnitude of the force
   ii the angle the force makes with the unit vector $\mathbf{i}$.

> **Hint** Draw a triangle of forces. Use Pythagoras' theorem to find the magnitude of the force and use trigonometry to find the angle.

a $(5\mathbf{i} + 2\mathbf{j})\,\text{N}$ **b** $(4\mathbf{i} - 3\mathbf{j})\,\text{N}$ **c** $\begin{pmatrix}-5\\4\end{pmatrix}\text{N}$ **d** $\begin{pmatrix}-6\\-2\end{pmatrix}\text{N}$

6 In this question, $\mathbf{i}$ represents the unit vector due east, and $\mathbf{j}$ represents the unit vector due north.

A particle is acted upon by forces of:

a $(5\mathbf{i} - 3\mathbf{j})\,\text{N}$, $(2\mathbf{i} + \mathbf{j})\,\text{N}$ and $(-3\mathbf{i} - 5\mathbf{j})\,\text{N}$

b $(3\mathbf{i} + 2\mathbf{j})\,\text{N}$, $(-4\mathbf{i} - 5\mathbf{j})\,\text{N}$ and $(4\mathbf{i} + 2\mathbf{j})\,\text{N}$

In each case, work out:
i the resultant vector
ii the magnitude of the resultant vector
iii the bearing of the resultant vector.

E/P 7 The forces $\mathbf{F}_1 = \begin{pmatrix}2a\\b\end{pmatrix}\text{N}$, $\mathbf{F}_2 = \begin{pmatrix}b\\-a\end{pmatrix}\text{N}$ and $\mathbf{F}_3 = \begin{pmatrix}-11\\1\end{pmatrix}\text{N}$ act on an object which is in equilibrium.

a Find the values of a and b. **(3 marks)**

The force $\mathbf{F}_3$ is removed. The resultant of the forces $\mathbf{F}_1$ and $\mathbf{F}_2$ is $\mathbf{R}$. **(2 marks)**

b Calculate, in newtons, the magnitude of $\mathbf{R}$.

c Calculate, to the nearest degree, the angle between the line of action of $\mathbf{R}$ and the unit vector $\mathbf{i}$. **(3 marks)**

P) 8 The forces $\mathbf{F}_1 = (4a\mathbf{i} + a\mathbf{j})\,\text{N}$, $\mathbf{F}_2 = (-2b\mathbf{i} - 8b\mathbf{j})\,\text{N}$ and $\mathbf{F}_3 = (-12\mathbf{i} + 12\mathbf{j})\,\text{N}$ act on an object which is in equilibrium.

a Find the values of a and b. **(3 marks)**

The force $\mathbf{F}_3$ is removed. The resultant of the forces $\mathbf{F}_1$ and $\mathbf{F}_2$ is $\mathbf{R}$.

b Calculate, in newtons, the magnitude of $\mathbf{R}$. **(2 marks)**

c Calculate, to the nearest degree, the angle between the line of action of $\mathbf{R}$ and the unit vector $\mathbf{j}$. **(3 marks)**

P) 9 A particle is acted upon by two forces $\mathbf{F}_1$ and $\mathbf{F}_2$, given by $\mathbf{F}_1 = (-4\mathbf{i} + 7\mathbf{j})\,\text{N}$ and $\mathbf{F}_2 = (2a\mathbf{i} - a\mathbf{j})\,\text{N}$, where a is a positive constant. The resultant of $\mathbf{F}_1$ and $\mathbf{F}_2$ is $\mathbf{R}$.

Given that $\mathbf{R}$ is parallel to $3\mathbf{i} + \mathbf{j}$, find the value of a. **(4 marks)**

10.3 Forces and acceleration

1 Find the acceleration when a particle of mass $250\,\text{kg}$ is acted on by a resultant force of $160\,\text{N}$.

> **Hint** Use Newton's second law of motion: $F = ma$

2 A $6\,\text{kg}$ object accelerates at a rate of $4\,\text{m s}^{-2}$ when a force is applied. Find the magnitude of the force.

3 Find the weight, in newtons, of a particle of mass $9\,\text{kg}$.

> **Hint** $W = mg$, where g is the acceleration due to gravity.

4 A box with mass $3\,\text{kg}$ is at rest on a smooth table. The box is pulled across the table by a horizontal string. The tension in the string has magnitude $0.9\,\text{N}$. Find:

> **Hint** In part **b**, use one of the *suvat* formulae. ← **Section 9.4**

a the acceleration of the box **b** the time taken to pull the box $15\,\text{m}$.

5 In each scenario, the forces acting on the body cause it to accelerate as shown. In each case, find the magnitude of the unknown force, P.

a   **b** 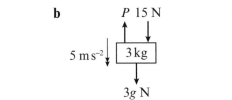   **c**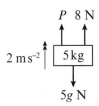

6 In each situation, the forces acting on the body cause it to accelerate as shown. Find the mass, m kg, of the body in each case.

a   **b** 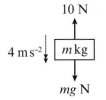   **c**

7 In each situation, the forces acting on the body cause it to accelerate as shown with magnitude $a\,\mathrm{m\,s^{-2}}$. In each case find the value of a.

a   30 N

$a\,\mathrm{m\,s^{-2}}$ ☐ 2 kg

      $2g$ N

b   15 N

$a\,\mathrm{m\,s^{-2}}$ ☐ 8 kg

      $8g$ N

c   50 N

$a\,\mathrm{m\,s^{-2}}$ ☐ 4 kg

      $4g$ N

(P) **8** A horizontal force of 40 N acts upon a particle of mass 5 kg, causing it to accelerate at $4\,\mathrm{m\,s^{-2}}$ along a rough horizontal plane. A constant resistive force opposes the motion of the particle. Calculate the magnitude of the resistive force.

9 An air-sea rescue crew member is suspended from a helicopter by a cable. The crew member has mass 60 kg. Find the tension in the cable when the crew member is being raised:

   a at a constant speed   **b** with an acceleration of $0.5\,\mathrm{m\,s^{-2}}$.

(E/P) **10** A lorry with mass 6000 kg accelerates uniformly from rest to a speed of $12\,\mathrm{m\,s^{-1}}$ in 10 seconds along a straight horizontal road. The lorry experiences a constant resistive force of 1800 N. Find:

   a the acceleration of the lorry   **(3 marks)**

   b the driving force provided by the engine of the lorry.   **(2 marks)**

(E/P) **11** A trolley with mass 60 kg is pulled in a straight line along a horizontal path by means of a horizontal rope attached to its front end. The trolley moves with a constant acceleration of $3.5\,\mathrm{m\,s^{-2}}$. The tension in the rope is 330 N and the trolley is subject to a constant resistive force of magnitude k N.

   a Find the value of k.   **(3 marks)**

At the instant the trolley is moving with speed $3\,\mathrm{m\,s^{-1}}$, the rope breaks.

   b Calculate how much further the trolley moves before coming to rest.   **(3 marks)**

10.4 Motion in 2 dimensions

In all the questions in this exercise, **i** represents the unit vector due east and **j** represents the unit vector due north.

1 A resultant force of $(6\mathbf{i} + \mathbf{j})$ N acts upon a particle of mass 4 kg.

   a Find the acceleration of the particle in the form $(p\mathbf{i} + q\mathbf{j})\,\mathrm{m\,s^{-2}}$.

> **Hint**   Use $\mathbf{F} = m\mathbf{a}$

   b Find the magnitude and bearing of the acceleration of the particle.

2 A resultant force of $(7\mathbf{i} + 2\mathbf{j})$ N acts on a particle of mass m kg causing it to accelerate at $(28\mathbf{i} + 8\mathbf{j})\,\mathrm{m\,s^{-2}}$. Work out the mass of the particle.

3 A particle of mass 5 kg is acted on by a force $\mathbf{F}$.
Given that the particle accelerates at $(10\mathbf{i} - 6\mathbf{j})\,\mathrm{m\,s^{-2}}$, find:

a an expression for $\mathbf{F}$ in the form $(p\mathbf{i} + q\mathbf{j})\,\mathrm{N}$

b the magnitude and bearing of $\mathbf{F}$.

> **Hint** Mass is a scalar quantity. This means that the acceleration of an object will be in the same direction as the line of action of the resultant force acting on the object.

4 Two forces, $\mathbf{F}_1$ and $\mathbf{F}_2$, act on a particle of mass m.
Find the acceleration of the particle, given that:

a $\mathbf{F}_1 = (3\mathbf{i} + 8\mathbf{j})\,\mathrm{N}$, $\mathbf{F}_2 = (-2\mathbf{i} + 3\mathbf{j})\,\mathrm{N}$, $m = 0.5\,\mathrm{kg}$

c $\mathbf{F}_1 = (-50\mathbf{i} - 40\mathbf{j})\,\mathrm{N}$, $\mathbf{F}_2 = (35\mathbf{i} + 15\mathbf{j})\,\mathrm{N}$, $m = 12\,\mathrm{kg}$

b $\mathbf{F}_1 = (8\mathbf{i} - 6\mathbf{j})\,\mathrm{N}$, $\mathbf{F}_2 = (3\mathbf{i} + 4\mathbf{j})\,\mathrm{N}$, $m = 7\,\mathrm{kg}$

d $\mathbf{F}_1 = 8\mathbf{i}\,\mathrm{N}$, $\mathbf{F}_2 = (-5\mathbf{i} - 10\mathbf{j})\,\mathrm{N}$, $m = 2.5\,\mathrm{kg}$

5 A particle of mass 5 kg is initially at rest. It is acted on by three forces: $\mathbf{F}_1 = (2\mathbf{i} + 5\mathbf{j})\,\mathrm{N}$, $\mathbf{F}_2 = (-\mathbf{i} - 6\mathbf{j})\,\mathrm{N}$ and $\mathbf{F}_3 = (3\mathbf{i} - 2\mathbf{j})\,\mathrm{N}$. Find:

a the magnitude and direction of the acceleration of the particle

b the time taken for the particle to reach a speed of $2\,\mathrm{m\,s^{-1}}$

c the speed of the particle after it has travelled 10 m.

> **Hint** For parts **b** and **c**, find the magnitude of the acceleration vector, then use the *suvat* formulae.

6 Two forces, $\begin{pmatrix} 1 \\ -5 \end{pmatrix}\,\mathrm{N}$ and $\begin{pmatrix} p \\ q \end{pmatrix}\,\mathrm{N}$, act on a particle P.

The resultant of the two forces is $\mathbf{R}$. Given that $\mathbf{R}$ acts in a direction which is parallel to the

vector $\begin{pmatrix} 1 \\ -2 \end{pmatrix}$, show that $2p + q - 3 = 0$. **(3 marks)**

7 A particle of mass 2.5 kg is being acted upon by three forces, $\mathbf{F}_1 = (3\mathbf{i} + 8\mathbf{j})\,\mathrm{N}$,
$\mathbf{F}_2 = (-7\mathbf{i} - 10\mathbf{j})\,\mathrm{N}$ and $\mathbf{F}_3 = (p\mathbf{i} + q\mathbf{j})\,\mathrm{N}$. Given that the particle is accelerating at a rate of
$(1.6\mathbf{i} - 2.4\mathbf{j})\,\mathrm{m\,s^{-2}}$, find the values of p and q. **(3 marks)**

8 A particle of mass 3 kg starts from rest and is acted upon by a force $\mathbf{R}$ of $(9\mathbf{i} + b\mathbf{j})\,\mathrm{N}$.
$\mathbf{R}$ acts on a bearing of $060°$.

a Find the value of b. **(1 mark)**

b Calculate the magnitude of $\mathbf{R}$. **(2 marks)**

c Work out the magnitude of the acceleration of the particle. **(2 marks)**

d Find the time taken for the particle to travel a distance of 75 m. **(3 marks)**

9 Three forces act on a particle: $\mathbf{F}_1 = (-4\mathbf{i} + 5\mathbf{j})\,\mathrm{N}$, $\mathbf{F}_2 = (-\mathbf{i} + 7\mathbf{j})\,\mathrm{N}$ and $\mathbf{F}_3 = (p\mathbf{i} + q\mathbf{j})\,\mathrm{N}$.

a Given that this particle is in equilibrium, determine the values of p and q. **(2 marks)**

Force $\mathbf{F}_2$ is removed.

b Given that in the first 10 seconds of its motion the particle travels a distance of 130 m, find the exact mass of the particle, in kg. **(3 marks)**

10 A particle of mass m kg is acted upon by forces of $(10\mathbf{i} + 8\mathbf{j})\,\mathrm{N}$, $(4\mathbf{i} + 12\mathbf{j})\,\mathrm{N}$ and $(-2\mathbf{i} - 4\mathbf{j})\,\mathrm{N}$,
causing it to accelerate at $5\,\mathrm{m\,s^{-2}}$. Work out the mass of the particle. **(3 marks)**

E/P **11** Two forces, $(6\mathbf{i} - 2\mathbf{j})$ N and $(p\mathbf{i} + q\mathbf{j})$ N, act on a particle of mass m kg. The resultant of the two forces is $\mathbf{R}$. Given that $\mathbf{R}$ acts in a direction which is parallel to the vector $(2\mathbf{i} + \mathbf{j})$,

    a find the angle between $\mathbf{R}$ and the vector $\mathbf{j}$ **(2 marks)**

    b show that $p - 2q + 10 = 0$.   **(4 marks)**

    c Given that $p = 4$ and that the particle moves with an acceleration of magnitude $2\sqrt{5}$ m s^{-2}, find the value of m.   **(7 marks)**

10.5 Connected particles

1 Two particles P and Q, of masses 6 kg and 10 kg respectively, are connected by a light inextensible string. The particles are on a smooth horizontal plane. A horizontal force of magnitude F is applied to P in a direction away from Q and when the string is taut the particles move with acceleration 0.4 m s^{-2}.

> **Hint** In part **a**, by considering the system as a single particle you eliminate the need to find the tension in the string.
>
> In part **b**, the particles need to be considered separately to find the tension in the string.

    a Find the value of F.   **b** Find the tension in the string.

2 Two particles P and Q, of masses 8 kg and m kg respectively, are connected by a light inextensible string. The particles are on a smooth horizontal plane. A horizontal force of 50 N is applied to Q in a direction away from P. When the string is taut the particles move with acceleration 2.5 m s^{-2}.

    a Find the value of m.   **b** Find the tension in the string.

3 Two particles P and Q, of masses 15 kg and 25 kg respectively, are connected by a light inextensible rod. The particles lie on a smooth horizontal plane. A horizontal force of 80 N is applied to Q in a direction towards P, causing the particles to move with acceleration a m s^{-2}.

> **Hint** The fact that the rod is inextensible means that both particles have the same acceleration.

    a Find the value of a.   **b** Find the thrust in the rod.

4 Two boxes A and B, of masses 150 kg and 250 kg respectively, sit on the floor of a lift of mass 2100 kg. Box A rests on top of box B. The lift is supported by a light inextensible cable and is descending with constant acceleration 1.2 m s^{-2}.

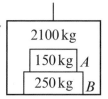

    a Find the tension in the cable.

    b Find the force exerted by box B on: **i** box A **ii** the floor of the lift.

5 A lorry of mass $2m$ kg is towing a trailer of mass $5m$ kg along a straight horizontal road. The lorry and trailer are connected by a light inextensible tow-bar. The lorry exerts a driving force of 60 000 N causing the lorry and trailer to accelerate at 4 m s^{-2}. The lorry and trailer experience resistances of 3200 N and 12 000 N respectively.

    a Find the mass of the lorry and hence the mass of the trailer.

    b Find the tension in the tow-bar.

6 Two particles A and B, of masses 16 kg and 9 kg respectively, are connected by a light inextensible string. Particle B hangs directly below particle A. A force of 250 N is applied vertically upwards to particle A, causing the particles to accelerate.

a Find the value of P. **(3 marks)**

b Find the tension in the string. **(2 marks)**

7 Two particles A and B, of masses 15 kg and 12 kg respectively, are connected by a light inextensible string. Particle B hangs directly below particle A. A force of P N is applied vertically upwards to particle A, causing the particles to accelerate at $2.5\,\mathrm{m\,s^{-2}}$.

a Find the magnitude of force P. **(3 marks)**

b Find the tension in the string. **(2 marks)**

8 A lorry of mass 3000 kg is towing a trailer of mass 5000 kg along a straight horizontal road. The lorry and trailer are connected by a light inextensible tow-bar. The lorry exerts a driving force of 72 000 N causing the lorry and trailer to accelerate at $4.5\,\mathrm{m\,s^{-2}}$. The lorry and trailer experience resistances of $2k$ N and $3k$ N respectively.

a Find the value of k. **(3 marks)**

b Find the tension in the tow-bar. **(2 marks)**

When the lorry and trailer are moving at $8\,\mathrm{m\,s^{-1}}$, the tow-bar breaks.

c Assuming that the driving force on the lorry and the resistances to motion are unchanged, find the distance travelled by the trailer before it comes to rest. **(6 marks)**

d State how you have used the modelling assumption that the tow-rope is inextensible. **(1 mark)**

9 A train consisting of an engine, mass 3200 kg, and a carriage, mass 1500 kg, moves along a straight horizontal track.

The engine is connected to the carriage by an inextensible shunt, which is parallel to the direction of motion of the train. The horizontal resistances to motion of the engine and the carriage have magnitudes 1000 N and 600 N respectively. The engine produces a constant horizontal driving force of magnitude 8650 N that causes the train to accelerate. Find:

a the acceleration of the train **(3 marks)**

b the magnitude of the tension in the shunt. **(3 marks)**

The train must stop at the next station, so the driver reduces the driving force to zero and applies the brakes. The brakes produce a constant force on the train of magnitude 2500 N, causing the engine and carriage to decelerate.

c Given that the other resistances to motion are unchanged, find the magnitude of the thrust in the shunt. Give your answer correct to 3 significant figures. **(7 marks)**

10.6 Pulleys

1 Particles A and B, of masses m and $3m$, are attached to the ends of a light inextensible string. The string is taut and passes over a small smooth fixed pulley. The system is released from rest.

   a i Write an equation of motion for A.   **ii** Write an equation of motion for B.

   b Find the magnitude of the acceleration of the particles. Give your answer in terms of g.

   c State how you have used the information that the string is inextensible.

E/P 2 Two particles have masses $4\,\text{kg}$ and $m\,\text{kg}$, where $m < 4$. They are attached to the ends of a light inextensible string. The string passes over a smooth fixed pulley. The particles are held in position with the string taut and the hanging parts of the string vertical.

The particles are then released from rest. The initial acceleration of each particle has magnitude $\frac{3}{13}g$. Find:

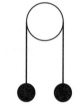

4 kg m kg

   a the tension in the string immediately after the particles are released   **(3 marks)**

   b the value of m.   **(3 marks)**

E/P 3 Two particles A and B, of masses $5\,\text{kg}$ and $2\,\text{kg}$ respectively, are connected by a light inextensible string, which is taut and passes over a smooth fixed pulley. The particles are released from rest.

   a Giving your answers in terms of g, find:

       i the acceleration of the system   **ii** the tension in the string.   **(4 marks)**

   When A has descended for 2.5 seconds it strikes the ground and immediately comes to rest.

   b Find the speed of A when it hits the ground.   **(3 marks)**

   c Assuming that B does not hit the pulley, find the greatest height that B reaches above its initial position.   **(3 marks)**

E/P 4 Two particles P and Q, of masses $6\,\text{kg}$ and $5\,\text{kg}$ respectively, are connected by a light inextensible string. Particle P lies on a rough horizontal table and the string passes over a small smooth pulley which is fixed at the edge of the table. Particle Q hangs freely.

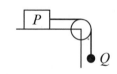

The friction between P and the table is $k\,\text{N}$. The system is released from rest and accelerates at a rate of $2\,\text{ms}^{-2}$. Find:

   a the tension in the string   **(4 marks)**

   b the value of k **(3 marks)**

   c the magnitude of the force exerted on the pulley by the string.   **(4 marks)**

E/P 5 Two particles A and B, of masses $2.8\,\text{kg}$ and $1.6\,\text{kg}$ respectively, are connected by a light inextensible string, which is taut. Particle A lies on a rough horizontal table, $2\,\text{m}$ from a small smooth pulley fixed at the edge. The string passes over the pulley and B hangs freely, $0.7\,\text{m}$ above ground. A frictional force of magnitude $0.5g\,\text{N}$ opposes the motion of particle A.

The system is released from rest. Find:

a the acceleration of the system   **(3 marks)**

b the time taken for B to reach the ground   **(4 marks)**

c the total distance travelled by A before it first comes to rest.   **(7 marks)**

Problem solving   Set A

Bronze

A car of mass 1200 kg is towing a trailer of mass 1000 kg along a straight horizontal road. The particles are connected by a tow-bar which is modelled as a light rod parallel to their direction of motion. The car is subject to a constant driving force of 4000 N. The resistances to the motion of the car and trailer are constant forces of magnitude 400 N and R N respectively.

The acceleration of the system is $1.5 \, \text{m s}^{-2}$.

a Show that $R = 300$.   **(3 marks)**

b Find the tension in the tow-bar.   **(3 marks)**

Silver

A train engine of mass 1300 kg is towing a carriage of mass 1100 kg along a straight horizontal track. The carriage is connected to the engine by a shunt, which is parallel to the direction of motion of the train. The train driver applies the brakes, which produces a force on the train of 400 N, and the train decelerates. The resistances to the motion of the engine and the carriage are modelled as constant forces of magnitudes 300 N and 500 N respectively.

a Find the time taken for the train to decelerate from $12 \, \text{m s}^{-1}$ to rest.   **(6 marks)**

b Comment on the assumption that the total resistances to motion are constant.   **(1 mark)**

Gold

A car of mass 1400 kg is towing a caravan of mass 1600 kg along a straight horizontal road. The caravan is connected to the car by a tow-bar which is parallel to the direction of motion of the car and caravan. The tow-bar is modelled as a light inextensible rod.

The driver brakes, producing a force on the car of F N, and the car and trailer decelerate. The resistances to the motion of the car and caravan are modelled as constant forces of magnitude 400 N and 600 N respectively. The magnitude of the thrust in the tow-bar is 200 N.

a Find the value of F.   **(6 marks)**

The model is refined to account for the mass of the tow-bar. The other values given in the question are unchanged.

b State how this will affect your answer to part **a**.   **(1 mark)**

Problem solving · Set B

Bronze

Two particles A and B have masses $2\,kg$ and $7\,kg$ respectively. The particles are connected by a light inextensible string which passes over a smooth light fixed pulley. The system is released from rest.

a i Write down an equation of motion for A.

  ii Write down an equation of motion for B. **(3 marks)**

b Find the acceleration. Give your answer in terms of g. **(1 mark)**

c State how you have used the information that the pulley is smooth. **(1 mark)**

Silver

Two particles A and B have masses $1\,kg$ and $5\,kg$ respectively. The particles are connected by a light inextensible string which passes over a smooth light fixed pulley. The particles are initially $0.75\,m$ above the ground. The system is released from rest. Assuming that B hits the ground before A reaches the pulley, find:

a the speed of B when it hits the ground **(6 marks)**

b the time taken for B to hit the ground. **(2 marks)**

Gold

Two particles A and B have masses $4\,kg$ and $6\,kg$ respectively. The particles are connected by a light inextensible string which passes over a smooth light fixed pulley. The system is released from rest. After descending $2\,m$, B strikes the ground and is immediately brought to rest. Given that A does not reach the pulley, find the distance travelled by A between the instant when B strikes the ground and the instant when the string next becomes taut. **(10 marks)**

Now try this → Exam question bank Q38, Q41, Q44, Q47, Q53, Q57, Q59, Q60

11.1 Functions of time

1 A particle P moves in a straight line. At time t seconds ($t \geqslant 0$), the displacement, s metres, of P from a point O is given by $s = 3t^3 - 2t^2$. Find:

a s when $t = 2$

b the time taken for the particle to return to O.

> **Hint** When the particle returns to O the displacement, $s = 0$.
>
> ← Section 9.3

2 A body moves in a straight line such that its velocity, v m s^{-1}, at time t seconds, is given by $v = 3t^2 - 14t + 8$ for $t \geqslant 0$. Find:

a the initial velocity

b the values of t when the body is instantaneously at rest

c the value of t when the velocity is 13 m s^{-1}

d the greatest speed of the body in the interval $0 \leqslant t \leqslant 3$.

> **Hint** For part **d**, sketch a velocity–time graph for the motion of the body and use the symmetric properties of the quadratic curve. **Speed** is the magnitude of the velocity, so the greatest speed could occur when the velocity is either positive or negative.
>
> ← Pure Year 1, Chapter 2

3 A particle P moves along the x-axis. At time t seconds, the displacement, s metres, is given by $s = 6t^2 - t^3$. Find:

a the change in displacement between $t = 3$ and $t = 5$

b the change in the displacement in the fourth second.

> **Hint** The fourth second is the time between $t = 3$ and $t = 4$.

4 At time $t = 0$, a toy train is at a point P. The train moves from point P in a straight line and then returns to P along the same straight line. Its distance from P, s m, at time t seconds can be modelled by

$$s = \tfrac{1}{4}(5t - t^2)$$

Find:

a the maximum distance of the train from P

b the time taken for the toy train to return to P

c the total distance travelled in this time

d the values of t for which the model is valid.

5 A particle P moves along the x-axis. At time t seconds ($t \geqslant 0$), the displacement, x metres, of P from the origin O is given by $x = 3t(t^2 - 4t + 4)$. Show that P will never move along the negative x-axis. **(2 marks)**

E/P **6** A particle P moves along the x-axis. At time t seconds the velocity of P is v m s^{-1} in the direction of x increasing, where $v = 2t^2 - 13t + 15$, $t \geqslant 0$. Find:

    a the times when P is instantaneously at rest   **(3 marks)**

    b the times when the velocity is 9 m s^{-1} **(3 marks)**

    c the greatest speed of P in the interval $0 \leqslant t \leqslant 5$.   **(5 marks)**

E/P **7** At time $t = 0$, a body moves in a straight horizontal line from a point O and then returns to its starting point. The displacement, s metres, from the point O at time t seconds is given by $s = 5t^2 - t^3$, $0 \leqslant t \leqslant T$.

    a Find the change in the displacement in the third second.   **(3 marks)**

    b Given that the model is valid when $s \geqslant 0$, find the value of T. Justify your answer.   **(3 marks)**

E/P **8** At time $t = 0$, a particle P leaves the origin O and moves along the x-axis. At time t seconds the velocity of P is v m s^{-1}, where $v = 10t - t^2$. Find:

    a the times when P is instantaneously at rest   **(2 marks)**

    b the maximum value of v.   **(4 marks)**

11.2 Using differentiation

1 Find the velocity of each particle at time $t = 2$, given that the particle's displacement (s metres) at time t seconds is given by:

> **Hint** Differentiate the expression for the displacement to find an expression for the velocity, then substitute $t = 2$ into that expression. The units of velocity will be m s^{-1}.

    a $s = 4t^3 - t$ **b** $s = 2t + t^2 - 1$

    c $s = t + t^{-1}$

2 Find an expression for **i** the velocity and **ii** the acceleration of a particle given that the displacement, s metres, at time t seconds is given by:

> **Hint** $v = \dfrac{\mathrm{d}s}{\mathrm{d}t}$, $a = \dfrac{\mathrm{d}v}{\mathrm{d}t} = \dfrac{\mathrm{d}^2 s}{\mathrm{d}t^2}$

    a $s = \dfrac{3t^4}{4} - \dfrac{1}{t^2}$

    b $s = (3t - 5)(2t^2 + 1)$

    c $s = \dfrac{2t^4 - 3t^2 + 8}{4t}$

3 A particle P is moving along the x-axis. At time t seconds the displacement, x metres, from O is given by $x = 2t^3 - 5t^2 + 8$, $t \geqslant 0$. Find:

    a the velocity of P when $t = 4$

    b the values of t for which P is instantaneously at rest

> **Hint** The particle is instantaneously at rest when $v = 0$.

    c the acceleration of P when $t = 2$.

4 A particle P is moving along the x-axis. At time t seconds (where $t \geqslant 0$), the velocity of P is v m s^{-1} in the direction of x increasing, where $v = 20 + t - t^2$. Find the acceleration of P when P is instantaneously at rest.

5 A particle P moves in a straight line. At time t seconds, the displacement, s cm, from a fixed point O is given by

$$s = \tfrac{1}{3}(2t^3 - 21t^2 + 60t + 90), \ t \geqslant 0$$

Find:

a the distance between the points at which the particle is instantaneously at rest **(7 marks)**

b the magnitude of the acceleration at these points. **(3 marks)**

6 A particle P moves along the x-axis. At time t seconds the velocity of P is v m s^{-1} in the direction of x increasing, where $v = 2t^2 - 17t + 21$, $t \geqslant 0$. Find:

a the times when P is instantaneously at rest **(3 marks)**

b the greatest speed of P in the interval $0 \leqslant t \leqslant 6$. **(5 marks)**

7 A particle P moves in a straight line. At time t seconds the displacement, s metres, is given by $s = kt^3 - 5t^2 + 12$, where k is a constant. When $t = 1$, the velocity of P is 8 m s^{-1}.

a Find the value of k. **(3 marks)**

b Hence find the magnitude of the acceleration when P is instantaneously at rest. **(5 marks)**

8 A particle P moves along a straight line. At time t seconds the velocity of P is v m s^{-1}, where

$$v = \tfrac{1}{10}t(8 - t)^2, \ 0 \leqslant t \leqslant 10$$

a Sketch a velocity–time graph for the motion of P. **(2 marks)**

b Find the values of t and the corresponding values of v when the acceleration of P is instantaneously zero. **(5 marks)**

11.3 Maxima and minima problems

1 A particle starts at a fixed point O and moves in a straight line before returning to O. The distance, s metres, from O at time t seconds is given by $s = 3t + 0.25t^2 - 0.25t^3$, $0 \leqslant t \leqslant 4$.

a Justify the restriction $0 \leqslant t \leqslant 4$.

b Find the maximum distance of the particle from O, correct to 3 significant figures.

> **Hint** For part **a**, find the roots of the cubic function and draw a sketch.
> ← **Pure Year 1, Section 4.1**
>
> For part **b**, look at your sketch. If the maximum distance occurs at a turning point, you can find the value of t by solving $\dfrac{ds}{dt} = 0$.
> ← **Pure Year 1, Section 12.9**

2 At time $t = 0$, a particle P leaves the origin, O, and moves along the x-axis. At time t seconds the velocity of P is v m s^{-1} where $v = t^2(t - 5)^2$, $0 \leq t \leq 6$.

   a Sketch a velocity–time graph for the motion of P.

   b Find the maximum value of v and the time at which it occurs.

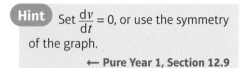

Hint Set $\frac{dv}{dt} = 0$, or use the symmetry of the graph.

← **Pure Year 1, Section 12.9**

3 A particle P moves in a straight line such that its distance, s metres, from a fixed point O at time t seconds is given by

$$s = 0.5t^3 - 0.45t^2 - 2.1t + 6, \ 0 \leq t \leq 4$$

The diagram shows the displacement–time graph of the motion of P.

   a Determine the time at which P is moving with minimum velocity.

   b Find the displacement of P from O at this time.

   c Find the velocity of P at this time.

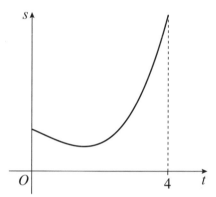

4 A body starts from rest and moves in a straight line. At time t seconds, the displacement of the body from the starting point, s metres, is given by $s = 5t^3 - t^4, 0 \leq t \leq 5$.

   a Find the time taken for the particle to return to the starting point.

   b Explain why s is always non-negative.

   c Find the maximum displacement of the body from its starting point.

(E) **5** A particle P moves in a straight line such that its displacement, s metres, from a fixed point O at time t seconds is given by $s = 0.5t^3 - 0.3t^2 - 0.8t + 6, 0 \leq t \leq 4$. Find the displacement of P from O when it is moving with minimum velocity. **(6 marks)**

(E/P) **6** A particle P moves along the x-axis. Its velocity, v m s^{-1}, in the positive x-direction at time t seconds is given by $v = 3t^2 - 6t + 8, t \geq 0$.

   a Show that P never comes to rest. **(2 marks)**

   b Find the minimum velocity of P. **(4 marks)**

(E/P) **7** An electric car moves in a straight line along a 5 km test track. The motion of the car is modelled as a particle travelling in a straight line, and the distance, s m, of the car from the start of the track after t seconds is given by $s = 4.8t + 1.2t^2 - 0.01t^3, 0 \leq t \leq 100$. Show that the car never reaches the end of the track. **(7 marks)**

(E/P) **8** A particle P moves in a straight line. The speed of P at time t seconds ($t \geq 0$) is v m s^{-1}, where $v = at^2 + bt + c$ and a, b and c are constants. When $t = 3$, the speed of P has its minimum value. When $t = 0$, $v = 28$ and when $t = 3$, $v = 1$.

Find the acceleration of P when $t = 4$. **(8 marks)**

11.4 Using integration

1 A particle is moving in a straight line. Given that $v = 0$ when $t = 0$, find an expression for the velocity of the particle if the acceleration is given by:

Hint $v = \int a\,dt$. Use the initial condition that $v = 0$ when $t = 0$ to find the constant of integration.

a $a = 4t^2 - 3t^3$

b $a = 5t + \dfrac{3t^2}{2}$

c $a = \dfrac{2t^3 - t^2}{t}$

2 A particle is moving in a straight line. Find:

   i an expression for the displacement of the particle

   ii the distance travelled by the particle in the first 3 seconds

when the velocity is given by:

Hint If the velocity is always positive in the interval $0 \leqslant t \leqslant 3$, then the distance travelled is given by the definite integral $\int_0^3 v\,dt$.

a $v = 2t^3 - \dfrac{t}{3} + 1$

b $v = \dfrac{t}{3}(2t^2 + t^3)$

c $v = 5t^2 + \dfrac{3\sqrt{t}}{2}$

3 A particle P is moving on the x-axis. At time t seconds, the velocity of P is $(10 + 3t - 2t^2)\,\text{m s}^{-1}$. At time $t = 0$, P is at the point where $x = 5$. Find the distance of P from O when $t = 2$.

4 A particle is moving in a straight line. At time t seconds its velocity, $v\,\text{m s}^{-1}$, is given by $v = 4t^2 - 20t + 21$. When $t = 0$, the displacement is 0. Find the distance between the two points where the particle is instantaneously at rest.

5 A particle P moves on the x-axis. The acceleration of P at time t seconds is $(t - 3)\,\text{m s}^{-2}$ in the positive x-direction. The velocity of P at time t seconds is $v\,\text{m s}^{-1}$. When $t = 0$, $v = 4$. Find:

a v in terms of t **(4 marks)**

b the values of t when P is instantaneously at rest **(3 marks)**

c the distance between the two points at which P is instantaneously at rest. **(4 marks)**

6 A particle P moves along the x-axis. At time t seconds ($t \geqslant 0$), the acceleration of P is $(5t + 9)\,\text{m s}^{-2}$ in the positive x-direction. When $t = 0$, the velocity of P is $3\,\text{m s}^{-1}$ in the positive x-direction. At time $t = T$, the velocity of P is $7\,\text{m s}^{-1}$ in the positive x-direction. Find the value of T.

(6 marks)

E/P **7** A particle P starts from rest at a fixed point O and moves in a straight line. At time t seconds the acceleration of P is proportional to $(5 - t^2)$, where $t \geq 0$, and the displacement of P from O is s metres. When $t = 2$, the velocity of P is 11 m s^{-1}.

Show that $s = \dfrac{t^2(30 - t^2)}{8}$ **(7 marks)**

E/P **8** A particle P moves in a straight line through a fixed point, O. The velocity of the particle, $v \text{ m s}^{-1}$ at time t seconds after passing through O is given by $v = 5 + 8t^2 - 2t^3$, $0 \leq t \leq 4$. The diagram shows a velocity–time graph of the motion of P.

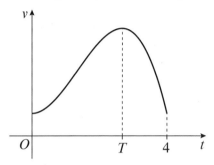

Find the distance of P from O at time T seconds, when the particle is moving with maximum velocity. **(7 marks)**

11.5 Constant acceleration formulae

1 A particle moves in a straight line such that its displacement, s metres, from a fixed point O at time t seconds is given by $s = ut + \frac{1}{2}at^2$, where u and a are constants. Use calculus to:

a find an expression for the velocity v in terms of u, a and t

b show that the acceleration is $a \text{ ms}^{-2}$.

> **Hint** For part **a**, use $v = \dfrac{\mathrm{d}s}{\mathrm{d}t}$
>
> For part **b**, use acceleration $= \dfrac{\mathrm{d}v}{\mathrm{d}t} = \dfrac{\mathrm{d}^2s}{\mathrm{d}t^2}$

2 A particle moves in a straight line with constant acceleration $a \text{ ms}^{-2}$. Given that when $t = 0$, the velocity is $u \text{ ms}^{-1}$ and the displacement is 0 m, find expressions in terms of u, a and t for:

a the velocity, $v \text{ ms}^{-1}$

b the displacement, $s \text{ m}$.

> **Hint** For part **a**, use $v = \int a \,\mathrm{d}t$.
>
> For part **b**, use $s = \int v \,\mathrm{d}t$.

3 Which of these equations for displacement describe constant acceleration? Explain your answers.

a $s = 3t - 2t^3$

b $s = t^2 - 7t$

c $s = \dfrac{5}{t} + 8$

d $s = 16 - \dfrac{t^2}{2}$

e $s = 10$

> **Hint** Check whether $\dfrac{\mathrm{d}^2s}{\mathrm{d}t^2}$ is a constant.

4 A car travels along a straight road. It passes through point A when $t = 0$ and through point B 50 seconds later. Its distance from A at time t seconds is given by $s = 32t - 0.3t^2$, $0 \leqslant t \leqslant 50$.

a Find the distance AB. **(1 mark)**

b Show that the car travels with constant acceleration. **(3 marks)**

5 A particle moves in a straight line with a constant acceleration of 3 m s^{-2}.

a Given that its initial velocity is 10 m s^{-1}, use calculus to show that its velocity at time t seconds is given by $v = 10 + 3t$. **(2 marks)**

b Given that the initial displacement of the particle is 5 m, show that $s = 10t + 1.5t^2 + 5$. **(3 marks)**

6 A particle moves in a straight line such that its displacement, s metres, from a fixed point O at time t seconds is given by $s = pt^2 + qt + r$, where p, q and r are constants. Given that when $t = 2$, $s = 8$, $v = 7$ and $a = 6$, find the values of p, q and r. **(5 marks)**

7 A particle moves in a straight line with constant acceleration. The initial displacement of the particle is 3 m and the initial velocity of the particle is 5 m s^{-1}. After 2 seconds it is moving with velocity 13 m s^{-1}. Find:

a the acceleration of the particle **(3 marks)**

b an equation for the displacement of the particle, s metres, in terms of t. **(5 marks)**

Problem solving Set A

Bronze

A particle P moves along the x-axis. At time t seconds ($t \geqslant 0$), the displacement, x metres, of P from the origin O is given by $x = t^3 - 8t^2 + 5t$. Find:

a the times when P is instantaneously at rest **(3 marks)**

b the distance between the two points at which P is instantaneously at rest **(4 marks)**

c the values of t for which the acceleration is positive. **(2 marks)**

Silver

A particle P moves along the x-axis. At time t seconds ($t \geqslant 0$), the displacement, x metres, of P from the origin O is given by $x = t(t^2 - 9t + 15)$. Find:

a the distance travelled by P in the negative x-direction **(6 marks)**

b the total distance travelled by P on the negative x-axis. **(2 marks)**

Gold

A particle P moves along the x-axis. At time t seconds ($t \geqslant 0$), the displacement, x metres, of P from the origin O is given by $x = \frac{1}{3}t^2(t^2 - 6t + 10)$.

a Show that P will never move along the negative x-axis. **(2 marks)**

Paula substitutes $t = 3$ into the expression for x and obtains an answer of 3. She states that the particle has moved a total distance of 3 m in the first three seconds of its motion.

b i Explain the mistake Paula has made.

   ii Determine the distance the particle travels in the first three seconds of its motion. **(7 marks)**

Problem solving   Set B

Bronze

A particle starts from a point, P, and moves in a straight line. At time t seconds after the beginning of its motion, the acceleration of the particle, a m s^{-2}, is given by $a = 5 - 2t$ for $t \geqslant 0$. When $t = 0$, $v = 6$ m s^{-2}. Find:

a the time when the particle is instantaneously at rest **(6 marks)**

b the displacement of the particle from P at this time. **(3 marks)**

Silver

A particle starts from rest and moves in a straight line from a point, P. At time t seconds after the beginning of its motion, the acceleration of the particle, a m s^{-2}, is given by $a = 9 - 6t$ for $0 \leqslant t \leqslant 3$. Find:

a the greatest speed of the particle **(6 marks)**

b the total distance travelled by the particle in the interval $0 \leqslant t \leqslant 3$. **(4 marks)**

Gold

A particle starts from rest and moves in a straight line from a point, P. At time t seconds after the beginning of its motion, the acceleration of the particle, a m s^{-2}, is given by $a = 26 - 12t$. Find:

a the total distance travelled by the particle in the first 5 seconds **(7 marks)**

b the time taken for the particle to return to P. **(5 marks)**

Now try this → **Exam question bank Q46, Q49, Q50, Q54, Q56, Q58**

Exam question bank

This bank of exam-style questions have not been ordered by topic. Read each question carefully to work out which skills and techniques you will need to apply.

Section A — Statistics

1   Alice wants to survey the students in her year group to find out their favourite type of animal. There are 75 boys and 85 girls in her year.
Explain briefly how Alice could take a random sample of 40 pupils using:

   a systematic sampling   **(2 marks)**

   b stratified sampling.   **(2 marks)**

2   A fair eight-sided dice is rolled 10 times.

   a Write down a suitable distribution for the random variable X, the number of times the dice shows an 8.   **(1 mark)**

   b Calculate: **i** $P(X = 1)$ **ii** $P(X \geqslant 2)$ **(3 marks)**

3   Eleri is investigating the daily total sunshine in Hurn during June 1987. She uses data from the first five days of the month.

   a Describe the sampling method used by Eleri.   **(1 mark)**

   b Suggest two alternative sampling methods and give one advantage and one disadvantage of each method in this context.   **(2 marks)**

   c State, with a reason, whether the data that Eleri has collected is discrete or continuous.   **(1 mark)**

4   Shania conducted a scientific experiment to measure the temperatures, $h\,°C$, generated by a chemical reaction and the amounts of a catalyst, $x\,g$, that was used in the reaction.

The smallest amount of catalyst she used was 1 g and the largest amount of catalyst she used was 30 g.

She calculated the regression line of h on x for her data and found it to be $h = 30 + 2.1x$.

   a Interpret the figures 30 and 2.1 in the context of the question.   **(2 marks)**

Shania decides to use her regression line to predict the temperature of the reaction if she uses 100 g of the catalyst.

   b Explain why it would not be sensible to do this.   **(1 mark)**

Her lab partner Monique uses the regression line to predict the amount of catalyst used when the temperature generated by the reaction is 60 °C.

   c Explain why it is not appropriate for Monique to do this.   **(1 mark)**

5 The daily mean temperatures, $t\,°C$, for a random sample of 20 days in Hurn during 2015 are taken from the large data set.

Temp, $t\,°C$	$8 \leqslant t < 10$	$10 \leqslant t < 12$	$12 \leqslant t < 14$	$14 \leqslant t < 16$	$16 \leqslant t < 18$
Frequency	2	7	4	5	2

© Crown Copyright Met Office

Two days from the sample are chosen at random.

a Find the probability that, on one of the two days, the temperature was between 12 °C and 14 °C. **(3 marks)**

b State one assumption you have made in calculating your answer to **a**. **(1 mark)**

6 A tomato farmer is investigating the ripeness and consistency of his crop. To test the ripeness of a tomato he picks and squeezes it.

a Explain why it would not be sensible for the farmer to use a census to test for ripeness. **(1 mark)**

He measures the consistency of the crop by weighing the tomatoes. He records the masses, to the nearest gram, of a random sample of tomatoes.

Mass (g)	110–119	120–129	130–139	140–149	150–159
Frequency	7	8	x	10	4

b Given that an estimate for the mean mass of a tomato from the sample is 133.5 g, find x. **(3 marks)**

c Calculate an estimate for the standard deviation of the masses. **(1 mark)**

A second farmer claims that her crop is more consistent in mass. She calculates the standard deviation of a random sample of 5 tomatoes and finds it to be 10.1 g.

d Comment on the validity of this claim. **(2 marks)**

7 A manufacturer of bicycle inner tubes wants to test the pressure at which the tubes burst.

a Explain why it would not be sensible for the manufacturer to use a census. **(1 mark)**

The manager decides to take a random sample of 5 inner tubes and measure the pressures at which they burst. The data, in kilopascals (kPa), is recorded below.

525 567 610 660 680

The manager says that the data supports packaging the inner tubes with a label which states: 'Inner tubes can withstand a pressure of at least 600 kPa.'

b Use the data above to suggest a reason why this labelling is not suitable. **(2 marks)**

c Suggest one way in which the manager can improve the reliability of the sampling. **(1 mark)**

8 The table shows the ages, t years, and the second-hand sale prices, y £1000s, of seven sports cars of the same model and specification at a particular dealership in one month.

Age, t years	0.1	0.5	0.8	1.1	1.4	1.5	1.7
Value, y £1000s	120	118	112	100	30	71	35

Elsbeth thinks a linear regression model is suitable for modelling this data. She calculates the equation of the regression line for y on t to be $y = 120 + 0.1t$.

a Explain how you know that Elsbeth has made a mistake with her regression line calculation. **(1 mark)**

b Assess Elsbeth's claim that a linear regression model is suitable for modelling this data. You must provide evidence for your conclusion. **(2 marks)**

One of the data points does not fit the general trend of the data.

c Suggest a possible reason why this might still be a valid data point. **(1 mark)**

9 In the large data set, daily mean cloud cover is measured in oktas.

a Explain what is meant by an 'okta'. **(1 mark)**

Harriet believes that the daily mean cloud cover in Hurn in 2015 can be modelled by the random variable X with probability mass function

$$P(X = x) = \tfrac{1}{8}, \qquad x = 1, 2, 3, 4, 5, 6, 7, 8$$

b State the type of distribution Harriet is using to model X. **(1 mark)**

c Use Harriet's distribution to find $P(X > 6)$. $\quad 0.25?$ **(1 mark)**

d Using your knowledge of the large data set, suggest a reason why Harriet's model might not be suitable. **(1 mark)**

10 Some students are interviewed to find the types of music they like.

Event A is 'likes rock music', event B is 'likes pop music' and event C is 'likes classical music'.

A Venn diagram is drawn to show the probabilities in this case.

a Write down a pair of events that are mutually exclusive. **(1 mark)**

b Write down the value of x. **(1 mark)**

c Show that events A and B are not statistically independent. **(2 marks)**

11 The box plots show the distributions of monthly daily mean temperatures, in °C, for Perth in 2015. The box plots are not in correct month order.

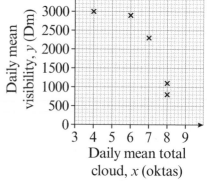

a Using your knowledge of the large data set, suggest which two box plots represent the distribution of daily mean temperatures for July and August. **(2 marks)**

b Explain what is meant by × in the box plots for months A and D. **(1 mark)**

c Estimate the number of days in month C that had a daily mean temperature greater than 20 °C. **(2 marks)**

12 Andrea is investigating the relationship between cloud cover and visibility. She takes a random sample of five days from the large data set for Hurn in May 1987. The table records her data.

Daily mean total cloud, x (oktas)	8	4	6	7	8
Daily mean visibility, y (Dm)	800	3000	2900	2300	1100

© Crown Copyright Met Office

a Using your knowledge of the large data set, explain what is meant by an 'okta'. State whether this variable is discrete or continuous. **(2 marks)**

Andrea draws a scatter diagram of this data.

She then calculates the equation of the regression line for y on x as $y = 5530 - 532x$.

b Suggest a reason why Andrea should not have used a linear regression model for this data. **(1 mark)**

c Suggest two more criticisms of Andrea's method. **(2 marks)**

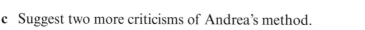

13 Naomi is interested in the amount of time, to the nearest hour, that people spend online during a typical week. By using opportunity sampling, she collects a sample of 25 people from shoppers on the high street.

a Explain what is meant by opportunity sampling. **(1 mark)**

b State, with a reason, whether the data that Naomi has collected is discrete or continuous. **(1 mark)**

Naomi's results are recorded in the table.

c Use linear interpolation to find an estimate of the interquartile range for this data. **(3 marks)**

Number of hours	Frequency
5–9	1
10–12	3
13–16	7
17–25	12
26–40	2

14 Ishika is taking part in a maths challenge which involves answering a series of multiple choice questions. Each question has four possible answers. Given that there are 25 questions in the challenge and Ishika guesses the answer to each one,

    a define a suitable distribution to model X, the number of questions that Ishika answers correctly   **(1 mark)**

    b find $P(X \geqslant 10)$.   **(2 marks)**

A teacher wants to set a pass mark such that the probability of a student passing the test by simply guessing answers is less than 5%.

    c State the lowest pass mark the teacher can set.   **(2 marks)**

15 Niamh is investigating the daily mean windspeed, in knots, in Perth in 2015. She wants to take a random sample of size 30 from all 194 dates in the large data set.

    a Explain briefly how Niamh could take her sample.   **(2 marks)**

The data that Niamh collects is summarised in the table.

Windspeed, w (kn)	$4 \leqslant w < 6$	$6 \leqslant w < 8$	$8 \leqslant w < 10$	$10 \leqslant w < 12$
Frequency	5	13	8	4

© Crown Copyright Met Office

    b Use linear interpolation to estimate the median daily mean windspeed.   **(2 marks)**

    c Use your calculator to find estimates for the mean and standard deviation of the daily mean windspeeds.   **(2 marks)**

16 The discrete random variable X has probability mass function

$$P(X = x) = \frac{k}{x}, \qquad x = 1, 2, 3$$

    a Find the value of k and write down, in table form, the probability distribution of X.   **(3 marks)**

Two independent observations are taken from X.

    b Find the probability that the second observation is larger than the first observation.   **(2 marks)**

17   **a** Explain what is meant by a sampling unit.   **(1 mark)**

    b Explain what is meant by a sampling frame.   **(1 mark)**

Manvitha is investigating the daily mean windspeed in Perth during 2015. She uses data from all 184 days in the large data set and decides to take a simple random sample of size 20.

    c Describe how Manvitha could take her sample.   **(2 marks)**

    d Give two advantages of using a simple random sample.   **(2 marks)**

18 Egg boxes each contain 24 eggs. The probability that an egg chosen from a box at random is cracked is 0.1.

a Define a suitable distribution to model the number of eggs, X, that are cracked in a particular box and state two assumptions that are necessary for this distribution to be valid. **(2 marks)**

A box is selected at random.

b Find the probability that in this box there are 2 or more cracked eggs. **(2 marks)**

A sample of 15 boxes is taken.

c Find the probability that there are exactly 9 boxes with 2 or more cracked eggs in. **(2 marks)**

19 Adrian is doing an experiment to find out whether there is a link between the pulse rate of a person after exercise and that individual's resting pulse rate.

He asks the first 10 students that he sees to take part in the experiment. He measures each student's resting pulse rate, x beats per minute, and also their pulse rate after exercise, y beats per minute.

a State the sampling method that Adrian has used. **(1 mark)**

The scatter diagram shows the results of Adrian's experiment.

b Describe the correlation between the pulse rate after exercise and the resting pulse rate.

(1 mark)

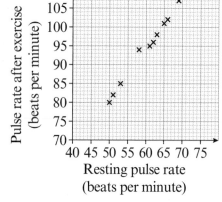

Adrian calculates the equation of the regression line for y on x as $y = 13.0 + 1.36x$.

c Explain why Adrian is justified in using a linear regression model for this data. **(1 mark)**

d Interpret the figure 1.36 in the context of the question. **(1 mark)**

e Explain why it would not be sensible for Adrian to use his equation to calculate the pulse rate after exercise for an 11th student whose resting pulse rate is 45 beats per minute.

(1 mark)

20 Subitsaa took a random sample of 30 daily mean windspeeds, in knots, from the large data set for Leeming in 2015. Her sample was stratified by month.

a State how many data values Subitsaa sampled from the data for July 2015.　**(2 marks)**

The data that Subitsaa collected is summarised in the table.

Windspeed, w (knots)	$4 \leqslant w < 6$	$6 \leqslant w < 8$	$8 \leqslant w < 10$	$10 \leqslant w < 12$
Frequency	8	9	6	7

© Crown Copyright Met Office

b Use linear interpolation to estimate the median and interquartile range in Subitsaa's sample of daily mean windspeeds.　**(2 marks)**

She took another random sample of daily mean windspeeds from the large data set for 30 days in Hurn in 2015. Her data is summarised in the box plot.

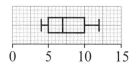

c Compare the distribution of daily mean windspeeds, in knots, for Leeming and Hurn.　**(2 marks)**

21 The table shows the daily mean windspeed, w knots, and the daily maximum gust, g knots in Leeming for a random sample of 9 days in 2015, taken from the large data set.

Windspeed, w (kn)	5	7	7	5	8	6	6	7	7
Max gust, g (kn)	18	19	19	18	31	18	17	21	19

© Crown Copyright Met Office

The median and quartiles for the maximum gust data are:

$Q_1 = 18$　　$Q_2 = 19$　　$Q_3 = 20$

An outlier is defined as a value which lies more than 1.5 × the interquartile range above the upper quartile or more than 1.5 × the interquartile range below the lower quartile.

a Show that $g = 31$ is an outlier.　**(1 mark)**

b Give a reason why you might exclude this day's readings.　**(1 mark)**

The data is cleaned and the regression line for g on w calculated for the remaining 8 data points. The equation of the regression line is found to be $g = 13.2 + 0.864w$.

c Interpret the meaning of the figures 13.2 and 0.864 in the context of the question.　**(2 marks)**

d Do you think there is a causal relationship between the daily mean windspeed and the daily maximum gust? Explain your reasoning.　**(1 mark)**

22 The cumulative frequency diagram shows the distribution of masses, in grams, of 100 loggerhead shrikes.

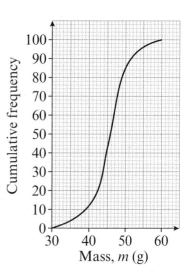

  a Estimate the median and interquartile range for this data.
  (3 marks)

  A team of ornithologists wants to catch, ring and release any of the birds that are heavier than 51 g.

  b Estimate the number of loggerhead shrikes that they need to catch. **(2 marks)**

  The box plot shows the distribution of masses, in grams, of 100 great grey shrikes.

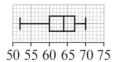

50 55 60 65 70 75

  The ornithologists want to catch, ring and release the same number of great grey shrikes as loggerhead shrikes. They estimate that the great grey shrikes have to have a mass greater than x g.

  c Use interpolation to calculate the value of x. **(2 marks)**

23 The traffic police in a town believe that 20% of impounded cars have illegal tyres.
A random sample of 30 cars from an impound lot is taken.

  a Give two reasons to support the use of a binomial distribution to model the random variable X, the number of cars in the sample that have illegal tyres. **(2 marks)**

  b Calculate the probability that the sample contains fewer than 4 cars with illegal tyres. **(2 marks)**

  The Department for Transport disagrees with the belief of the police and claims that the percentage of impounded cars with illegal tyres is less than 20%.

  c Write down suitable null and alternative hypotheses that can be used to test this claim. **(2 marks)**

  The Department for Transport tests its claim using a 10% level of significance.

  d Given that there were 3 cars in the sample that had illegal tyres, comment on the Department for Transport's claim. **(2 marks)**

24 Hafsah is investigating the daily mean pressure, x hPa, in Jacksonville in 1987. She takes a random sample of size 10 from the large data set.

  Hafsah codes the data using $y = \dfrac{x - 1010}{4}$

  Summary statistics for the coded data are:

  $$\sum y = 21 \qquad \sum y^2 = 44.625$$

a Calculate the mean and variance of the coded data. **(3 marks)**

b Use your answer to part **a** to find the mean and standard deviation of the data in Hafsah's sample. **(2 marks)**

Mishel says that Hafsah's results are unreliable.

c Suggest a way in which Hafsah can improve the reliability of her results. **(1 mark)**

25 A supermarket has three different suppliers for its oranges. Supplier X supplies 20% of the oranges and it is found that 3% of these oranges are spoilt on arrival. Supplier Y supplies 40% of the oranges and it is found that 4% of these oranges are spoilt on arrival. The remaining oranges are supplied by supplier Z.

Overall, 5% of the oranges received by the supermarket are spoilt on arrival.

a Find the percentage of oranges from supplier Z that are spoilt on arrival. **(3 marks)**

b Show that the event 'orange is from supplier X' and the event 'orange is spoilt on arrival' are not statistically independent. **(4 marks)**

26 The histogram shows the distribution of the times taken, in hours, for 1000 athletes to complete a marathon.

The runners qualify for the national championships if they finish the marathon in less than 2 hours and 36 minutes.

a Estimate the number of runners who qualified for the championships. **(3 marks)**

b Estimate the mean and standard deviation of the times taken. **(4 marks)**

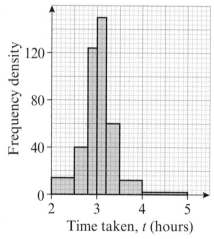

27 The head of sixth form suggests that the probability that Savannah is late to school is 0.3. Savannah does not believe this and, to test the claim, she records the number of days she is late over a random sample of 25 days.

a Define the term 'critical region' in the context of hypothesis testing. **(1 mark)**

b Find the critical region for a two-tailed test, at the 5% level of significance, to test whether the probability Savannah is late to school is 0.3. The probability of rejecting each tail should be as close as possible to 2.5%. **(4 marks)**

c State the actual significance level of the test. **(1 mark)**

From the sample, Savannah finds that she was late on 4 occasions.

d Comment on whether Savannah should accept the head of sixth form's claim in light of this evidence. **(2 marks)**

28 A bag contains a large number of identical-sized coloured disks.

In the bag, 58% of the disks are blue, 22% of the disks are green and the rest are yellow.

A random sample of 30 disks is taken from the bag.

a Explain why it is appropriate to model the random variable 'number of yellow disks in the sample' using a binomial distribution. **(2 marks)**

b Find the probability that the sample contains at least 7 yellow disks. **(2 marks)**

All of the disks are replaced and the experiment is repeated.

c Find the probability that there are at least 7 yellow disks on one occasion and fewer than 7 on the other. **(3 marks)**

29 A random variable X has distribution $B(15, p)$.

Amy uses a single observation of X to test H_0: $p = 0.34$ against H_0: $p \neq 0.34$.

a Using a 10% level of significance, find the critical region for Amy's test. The probability in each tail should be as close as possible to 0.05. **(3 marks)**

b Write down the actual significance level of Amy's test. **(2 marks)**

Donna decides to take two independent observations of X and reject H_0 only if both of her observations fall within the critical region.

c State, with a reason, whether the actual significance level of Donna's test is larger or smaller than Amy's. **(1 mark)**

30 A teacher is investigating the times taken, t minutes, for her class to complete a maths quiz. She produces a table of coded times, x minutes, for a random sample of 32 students.

Coded time (x minutes)	Frequency (f)	Coded time midpoint (y minutes)
$0 \leqslant x < 2$	3	1
$2 \leqslant x < 5$	11	3.5
$5 \leqslant x < 10$	7	7.5
$10 \leqslant x < 15$	8	12.5
$15 \leqslant x < 20$	3	17.5

You are given these summary statistics:

$$\sum fy = 246.5 \qquad \sum fy^2 = 2700.25$$

a Use linear interpolation to estimate the median of the coded times. **(2 marks)**

b Estimate the standard deviation of the coded times. **(2 marks)**

The head of department is told by the teacher that she subtracted 10 from each of the times and then divided by 2 to calculate the coded times.

c Calculate an estimate for the median and standard deviation of the actual times. **(2 marks)**

In a different quiz, students can qualify for a national competition. There are a maximum of 10 places available, and students must complete the quiz in 16 minutes or less to qualify. 45 Students take part in the quiz.

d Will the teacher fill all of the places available? Give a reason for your answer. **(2 marks)**

31 Charlie is playing a game with her friend Mikhela. The probability of her winning any one game is 0.2. Charlie and Mikhela play the game 25 times.

a Find the probability that Charlie wins exactly 6 of the games. **(1 mark)**

b Find the probability that Charlie wins more than 8 games. **(2 marks)**

Charlie claims that she has a trick that she can use to increase her probability of winning. To test the claim, Charlie and Mikhela play the game 25 more times and Charlie wins 9 times.

c Write down suitable null and alternative hypotheses for this test. **(2 marks)**

d Using a significance level of 5% and your answer to part **b**, state the outcome of the test. You must justify your answer. **(2 marks)**

32 The daily mean windspeeds, w knots, for a random sample of 30 days in Camborne in 2015 are taken from the large data set.

Wind speed, w (kn)	$5 \leqslant w < 8$	$8 \leqslant w < 11$	$11 \leqslant w < 14$	$14 \leqslant w < 17$	$17 \leqslant w < 20$
Frequency	7	5	6	8	4

© Crown Copyright Met Office

a Calculate estimates for the mean and standard deviation for this data. **(2 marks)**

b Calculate an estimate for the probability that the daily mean windspeed on a day chosen from the sample at random was greater than one standard deviation from the mean. **(3 marks)**

c State one assumption that you have made in calculating your answer to part **b**. **(1 mark)**

33 A sample of students are asked how many pets they have and the following probability distribution is generated, where X is the discrete random variable 'number of pets'.

x	1	2	3	4	5
$P(X = x)$	a	0.15	$2a$	0.2	0.1

a Calculate the value of a. **(2 marks)**

b Find the minimum number of students that were surveyed. Give a reason for your answer. **(2 marks)**

c Two students are chosen at random from the sample. Find the probability that:

i both students have 2 pets

ii between the two students, the total number of pets is 5. **(4 marks)**

34 From the large data set, the probability of a randomly chosen day in Camborne in 1987 having 7 or 8 oktas of cloud cover is 0.36.

Maedeh believes the likelihood getting 7 or 8 oktas of cloud cover increased in 2015. She decides to take a random sample of 42 days from the large data set for Camborne in 2015, stratified by month.

  a Explain briefly how Maedeh could take her sample. **(2 marks)**

  b State what is meant by a null hypothesis. **(1 mark)**

  c Write down two suitable hypotheses that Maedeh can use to test her belief. **(1 mark)**

From her sample, she finds that there are 7 or 8 oktas of cloud cover on 22 days.

  d Using a 5% level of significance, test whether or not there is evidence supporting Maedeh's belief. **(4 marks)**

35 Genevieve took a stratified random sample of size 50 from the students in her school. She used the different year groups as her strata.

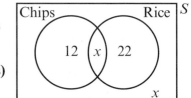

  a Explain briefly how Genevieve took her sample. **(2 marks)**

She asked each of the students in the sample if they liked chips or rice.

She summarised her findings in a Venn diagram.

  b Write down the value of x. **(1 mark)**

One student from the sample is chosen at random.

  c Calculate the probability that they like either chips or rice, or both. **(2 marks)**

  d Are the events 'like chips' and 'like rice' independent? Justify your answer. **(3 marks)**

36 Tanvi is researching the distances travelled by people to her local church. She stands outside the door of the church on Sunday between 10 am and 10:30 am and asks the first 20 people, as they arrive, how far they have travelled.

  a State the sampling method Tanvi has used. **(1 mark)**

  b State and briefly describe an alternative non-random sampling method that Tanvi could have used to collect her sample of 20 people. **(2 marks)**

Spardha decides to ask every person that attends church on Sunday the distance, x km, that they have travelled.

  c State the data selection process that Spardha has used. **(1 mark)**

Spardha's results are summarised by the box plot and summary statistics below.

$n = 50$, $\sum x = 385$, $\sum x^2 = 3517$

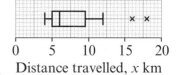

Distance travelled, x km

d Write down the interquartile range for these data. **(1 mark)**

e Calculate the mean and standard deviation for these data. **(3 marks)**

f State, giving a reason, whether you would recommend using the mean and standard deviation, or the median and interquartile range, to describe these data. **(2 marks)**

Joan and Esha both attend the church and have moved house since Spardha collected her data. Joan's journey has changed from a distance of 4.5 km to 9 km and Esha's journey has changed from a distance of 4.8 km to 8 km.

Spardha redrew her box plot and only had to change two values.

g Explain which two values Spardha had to change and whether they had increased or decreased. **(3 marks)**

Section B   Mechanics

37 A car accelerates along a straight road. The car passes a road sign A, and then 30 seconds later passes a second road sign B. The distance from A to B is 750 m.

The car is modelled as a particle moving with constant acceleration.

Given that the speed of the car at B is $42\,\text{m s}^{-1}$, find:

a the acceleration of the car **(2 marks)**

b the speed of the car at A. **(2 marks)**

38 Two particles A and B of masses 10 kg and m kg respectively are connected by a light inextensible string. Particle B hangs directly below particle A. A force of 150 N is applied vertically upwards to particle A, causing the particles to accelerate at $3\,\text{m s}^{-2}$.

a Find the value of m. **(3 marks)**

b Find the tension in the string. **(2 marks)**

39 A particle is travelling with velocity $20\,\text{m s}^{-1}$. At point A the particle accelerates at a constant rate, reaching a velocity of $k\,\text{m s}^{-1}$ after 40 seconds. The particle then immediately decelerates a constant rate, coming to rest at point B after a further 20 seconds.

a Sketch a velocity–time graph to illustrate the motion. **(3 marks)**

Given that the distance between A and B is 1120 m,

b find the value of k. **(3 marks)**

40 A particle is moving on the x-axis with constant deceleration $0.75\,\text{m s}^{-2}$. At time $t = 0$, the particle passes through the origin O, moving in the positive x-direction with speed $12\,\text{m s}^{-1}$. The particle reaches point A and then returns to O. Find:

   a the distance OA **(2 marks)**

   b the range of values for t for which the displacement from O is greater than $42\,\text{m}$. **(4 marks)**

41 Two forces, $\begin{pmatrix} -1 \\ 3 \end{pmatrix}\text{N}$ and $\begin{pmatrix} p \\ q \end{pmatrix}\text{N}$, act on a particle P.

   The resultant of the two forces is $\mathbf{R}$. Given that $\mathbf{R}$ acts in a direction which is parallel to the vector $\begin{pmatrix} 3 \\ -4 \end{pmatrix}$, show that $4p + 3q + 5 = 0$. **(4 marks)**

42 A car travels along a straight test track with constant acceleration. Three posts, P, Q and R, are fixed in that order at the side of the track.

   The car passes post P travelling with a velocity of $6\,\text{m s}^{-1}$, then passes post Q one minute later with a velocity of $18\,\text{m s}^{-1}$.

   a Find:

      i the distance from P to Q

      ii the velocity of the car 30 seconds after it passes post P. **(5 marks)**

   Given that the ratio of the distances $PQ : QR = 3 : 2$,

   b find the time taken for the car to travel from Q to R. **(3 marks)**

43 A car starts from rest at a signpost A and moves along a straight horizontal road. The car decelerates uniformly at a rate of $0.8\,\text{m s}^{-2}$ from a speed of $21\,\text{m s}^{-1}$ to a speed of $13\,\text{m s}^{-1}$. The speed is then maintained for $520\,\text{m}$. Finally, the car decelerates uniformly for 20 seconds before coming to rest at B.

   a For this journey from A to B, find:

      i the total time taken   **ii** the distance from A to B. **(5 marks)**

   b Sketch a displacement–time graph for the motion of the car, showing clearly the shape of the graph for each stage of the journey. **(3 marks)**

44 A car with mass $1800\,\text{kg}$ accelerates from rest to a speed of $12\,\text{m s}^{-1}$ in 8 seconds along a horizontal road. The car experiences a constant resistive force of $1400\,\text{N}$. Find:

   a the acceleration of the car **(3 marks)**

   b the driving force provided by the engine of the car. **(2 marks)**

   c Comment on the assumption that the total resistances to motion are constant. **(1 mark)**

45 A ball is projected upwards from a point which is x m above the ground with speed $12\,\text{m}\,\text{s}^{-1}$. The ball is modelled as a particle moving vertically under gravity. Given that the ball hits the ground 3 seconds after it is projected,

  a find the value of x. **(4 marks)**

  In a refined model of the motion of the ball, the effect of air resistance is included. The speed of projection and the total time of flight are unchanged. This refined model is now used to find the value of x.

  b How would this new value of x compare with the value found using the initial model in part **a**? **(1 mark)**

46 A particle P moves along the x-axis. At time t seconds the velocity of P is $v\,\text{m}\,\text{s}^{-1}$ in the positive x-direction, where $v = 2t^2 - 3t + 4$. When $t = 0$, P is at the origin O. Find the distance of P from O when P is moving with minimum velocity. **(8 marks)**

47 A particle of mass $0.8\,\text{kg}$ lies at rest in a horizontal plane, acted upon by three forces

$$\mathbf{F}_1 = \begin{pmatrix} a \\ b \end{pmatrix}\text{N}, \mathbf{F}_2 = \begin{pmatrix} b \\ -2a \end{pmatrix}\text{N} \text{ and } \mathbf{F}_3 = \begin{pmatrix} -7 \\ 8 \end{pmatrix}\text{N}$$

  a Find the values of a and b. **(3 marks)**

  The force $\mathbf{F}_3$ is removed. The resultant of the forces $\mathbf{F}_1$ and $\mathbf{F}_2$ is $\mathbf{R}$. **(2 marks)**

  b Calculate, in newtons, the exact magnitude of $\mathbf{R}$.

  c Calculate, to the nearest degree, the angle between the line of action of $\mathbf{R}$ and the unit vector $\mathbf{i}$. **(3 marks)**

  d Find the distance travelled by the particle in the first 3 seconds after the force $\mathbf{F}_3$ is removed. **(3 marks)**

48 A ball is projected vertically upwards with speed $14\,\text{m}\,\text{s}^{-1}$ from a point A, which is $3.6\,\text{m}$ above the ground. Find:

  a the greatest height above A reached by the ball **(3 marks)**

  b the speed of the ball as it strikes the ground **(3 marks)**

  c the time between the instant when the ball is projected from A and the instant when the ball strikes the ground. **(3 marks)**

49 A particle P moves along a straight line. The speed of P at time t seconds ($t \geqslant 0$) is $v\,\text{m}\,\text{s}^{-1}$, where $v = (pt^2 + qt + r)$ and p, q and r are constants. When $t = 3$, the speed of P has its minimum value. When $t = 0$, $v = 10$ and when $t = 2$, $v = 5$. Find:

  a the acceleration of P when $t = 4$ **(8 marks)**

  b the distance travelled by P in the third second of the motion. **(5 marks)**

50 A car travels in a straight line. It passes through a point A when $t = 0$ and through a point B when $t = 30$. Its distance from A at time t seconds is given by $s = 25t - 0.3t^2$, $0 \leqslant t \leqslant 30$.

A second car travels in the opposite direction along the same road as the first car. It passes through B when $t = 0$ with an initial velocity of $15\,\text{m s}^{-1}$ and travels directly towards A with a constant acceleration of $0.1\,\text{m s}^{-2}$. Find:

a the distance AB **(2 marks)**

b the distance from A at which the two cars pass one another. **(8 marks)**

51 A particle is moving in a straight horizontal line with constant deceleration $3\,\text{m s}^{-2}$. At time $t = 0$ the particle passes through a point O with speed $18\,\text{m s}^{-1}$ and is travelling towards a point A, where $OA = 48\,\text{m}$. Find:

a the times when the particle passes through A **(4 marks)**

b the value of t when the particle returns to O. **(3 marks)**

52 A small ball is dropped from a height of $10\,\text{m}$ onto level ground. It strikes the ground and bounces. The speed of the ball at the instant after it bounces is half its speed at the instant before it bounces. It rebounds to a height of $x\,\text{m}$, before falling again to the ground. The motion of the ball is modelled as that of a particle moving freely under gravity.

a i Find the value of x

ii Find the total time that elapses between when the ball is dropped and when it hits the ground for the second time. **(4 marks)**

The model is refined to include air resistance, which is modelled as a constant resistive force of magnitude $0.5\,\text{N}$. Given that the mass of the ball is 0.2 kg,

b find the speed of the ball immediately before it bounces **(5 marks)**

c state, without calculation, how the value of x will differ to that found in part **a i** and give a reason for your answer. **(1 mark)**

53 Block P, of mass 0.5 kg, sits on a rough horizontal table. A light inextensible string passes over a smooth pulley and is attached to block P at one end and a light scale pan at the other, as shown. The scale pan carries two blocks A and B, of mass 0.2 kg and 0.8 kg respectively, with A on top of B. The total resistance to motion of P is modelled as a force of constant magnitude $2\,\text{N}$.

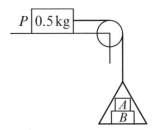

a i Write an equation of motion for P.

ii Write an equation of motion for the scale pan. **(4 marks)**

b Hence find the:

i magnitude of the tension in the string **ii** acceleration of P. **(3 marks)**

c Find the magnitude of the force exerted by block B on block A. **(3 marks)**

d State how you have used the fact that the pulley is smooth in your calculations. **(1 mark)**

54 A particle moves in a straight line. At time t seconds, the particle's displacement, s m, is given as $s = (2 - t)^4$, $t \geqslant 0$. Show that:

    a $v \geqslant 0$ when $t \geqslant k$ (where v is the particle's velocity in $\mathrm{m\,s^{-1}}$) and state the least possible value of k.   **(5 marks)**

    b   the acceleration, $a\,\mathrm{m\,s^{-2}}$, can be written as $a = 12(t - 2)^2$.   **(4 marks)**

55 The velocity–time graph models the motion of a sprinter running a 100 m race. The sprinter accelerates uniformly from rest for 2 seconds, then travels at a constant speed of $12\,\mathrm{m\,s^{-1}}$ for 6.5 seconds, before accelerating uniformly to the finish line at a rate of $1.5\,\mathrm{m\,s^{-2}}$.

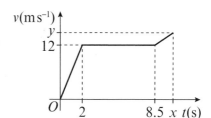

    a   Find, correct to 3 significant figures:

        i   the total length of time the sprinter takes to finish the race, x seconds

        ii   the speed of the sprinter as he crosses the finish line, $y\,\mathrm{m\,s^{-1}}$.   **(7 marks)**

    b   With reference to the velocity–time graph, give one criticism of the model of the sprinter's motion.   **(1 mark)**

56 A particle moves in a straight line. At time t seconds, the acceleration of the particle, $a\,\mathrm{m\,s^{-2}}$, is given by $a = 3 - \dfrac{2}{t^3}$

When $t = 1$, the particle is at rest at a fixed point P on the line. Find, in terms of t:

    a   an expression for the velocity of the particle   **(5 marks)**

    b   an expression for the displacement, s m, of the particle from P.   **(5 marks)**

57 Two particles A and B have masses $4\,\mathrm{kg}$ and $m\,\mathrm{kg}$ respectively, where $m < 4$. The particles are connected by a light inextensible string which passes over a smooth light fixed pulley. The system is held at rest with the string taut. The hanging parts of the string are vertical and A and B are at the same height above a horizontal plane.

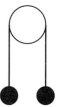

The system is released from rest and A descends with acceleration $\frac{3}{5}g\,\mathrm{m\,s^{-2}}$. $4\,\mathrm{kg}$ $m\,\mathrm{kg}$

    a   Find the tension in the string.   **(3 marks)**

    b   Find the value of m.   **(3 marks)**

After descending for 0.6 seconds, particle A reaches the plane and is immediately brought to rest by the impact. The initial distance between B and the pulley is such that B never reaches the pulley.

    c   Find the greatest height reached by B above the plane, to 3 significant figures.   **(7 marks)**

58 A particle moves in a straight line with acceleration $a\,\text{m}\,\text{s}^{-2}$. At any time, t seconds, a is inversely proportional to t^3. When $t = 1$, the velocity of the particle is $2\,\text{m}\,\text{s}^{-1}$. Given the velocity approaches a limiting value of $6\,\text{m}\,\text{s}^{-1}$, find an expression for the velocity at any time t. **(9 marks)**

59 Particle A of mass $3\,\text{kg}$ lies on a smooth horizontal table which is $1.3\,\text{m}$ above the floor. A light inextensible string of length $1\,\text{m}$ connects A to a particle B of mass $2\,\text{kg}$. The string passes over a smooth pulley which is fixed to the edge of the table and B hangs vertically $0.5\,\text{m}$ below the pulley.

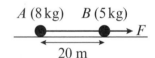

The system is released from rest.

a Find the magnitude of the force exerted on the pulley. **(7 marks)**

b Find the speed with which A hits the pulley. **(3 marks)**

c State how you have used the fact that the pulley is smooth in your calculations. **(1 mark)**

When A hits the pulley, the string breaks and B falls to the ground.

d Find the time between the instant that the string breaks and the instant when B strikes the ground. **(4 marks)**

60 Two particles A and B of masses $8\,\text{kg}$ and $5\,\text{kg}$ respectively are initially at rest on a rough horizontal surface. They are joined by a light inextensible string of length $20\,\text{m}$. A constant force F of magnitude $300\,\text{N}$ is applied for 2 seconds, during which time particle B travels a distance of $28.8\,\text{m}$.

The total resistances to motion acting on each particle are modelled as being constant and of magnitude $k\,\text{N}$ (so that the total resistance to motion of the whole system has magnitude $2k\,\text{N}$).

a Find the value of k. **(5 marks)**

b Find the magnitude of the tension in the string. **(3 marks)**

c State how you have used the fact that the string is inextensible in your calculations. **(1 mark)**

After 2 seconds, the force F is removed and the particles continue to travel in the same straight line.

d Show that, in the subsequent motion, particle A will collide with particle B. **(7 marks)**

Binomial cumulative distribution function

The tabulated value is $P(X \leq x)$, where X has a binomial distribution with index n and parameter p.

$p =$	0.05	0.10	0.15	0.20	0.25	0.30	0.35	0.40	0.45	0.50
$n = 5, x = 0$	0.7738	0.5905	0.4437	0.3277	0.2373	0.1681	0.1160	0.0778	0.0503	0.0312
1	0.9774	0.9185	0.8352	0.7373	0.6328	0.5282	0.4284	0.3370	0.2562	0.1875
2	0.9988	0.9914	0.9734	0.9421	0.8965	0.8369	0.7648	0.6826	0.5931	0.5000
3	1.0000	0.9995	0.9978	0.9933	0.9844	0.9692	0.9460	0.9130	0.8688	0.8125
4	1.0000	1.0000	0.9999	0.9997	0.9990	0.9976	0.9947	0.9898	0.9815	0.9688
$n = 6, x = 0$	0.7351	0.5314	0.3771	0.2621	0.1780	0.1176	0.0754	0.0467	0.0277	0.0156
1	0.9672	0.8857	0.7765	0.6554	0.5339	0.4202	0.3191	0.2333	0.1636	0.1094
2	0.9978	0.9842	0.9527	0.9011	0.8306	0.7443	0.6471	0.5443	0.4415	0.3438
3	0.9999	0.9987	0.9941	0.9830	0.9624	0.9295	0.8826	0.8208	0.7447	0.6563
4	1.0000	0.9999	0.9996	0.9984	0.9954	0.9891	0.9777	0.9590	0.9308	0.8906
5	1.0000	1.0000	1.0000	0.9999	0.9998	0.9993	0.9982	0.9959	0.9917	0.9844
$n = 7, x = 0$	0.6983	0.4783	0.3206	0.2097	0.1335	0.0824	0.0490	0.0280	0.0152	0.0078
1	0.9556	0.8503	0.7166	0.5767	0.4449	0.3294	0.2338	0.1586	0.1024	0.0625
2	0.9962	0.9743	0.9262	0.8520	0.7564	0.6471	0.5323	0.4199	0.3164	0.2266
3	0.9998	0.9973	0.9879	0.9667	0.9294	0.8740	0.8002	0.7102	0.6083	0.5000
4	1.0000	0.9998	0.9988	0.9953	0.9871	0.9712	0.9444	0.9037	0.8471	0.7734
5	1.0000	1.0000	0.9999	0.9996	0.9987	0.9962	0.9910	0.9812	0.9643	0.9375
6	1.0000	1.0000	1.0000	1.0000	0.9999	0.9998	0.9994	0.9984	0.9963	0.9922
$n = 8, x = 0$	0.6634	0.4305	0.2725	0.1678	0.1001	0.0576	0.0319	0.0168	0.0084	0.0039
1	0.9428	0.8131	0.6572	0.5033	0.3671	0.2553	0.1691	0.1064	0.0632	0.0352
2	0.9942	0.9619	0.8948	0.7969	0.6785	0.5518	0.4278	0.3154	0.2201	0.1445
3	0.9996	0.9950	0.9786	0.9437	0.8862	0.8059	0.7064	0.5941	0.4770	0.3633
4	1.0000	0.9996	0.9971	0.9896	0.9727	0.9420	0.8939	0.8263	0.7396	0.6367
5	1.0000	1.0000	0.9998	0.9988	0.9958	0.9887	0.9747	0.9502	0.9115	0.8555
6	1.0000	1.0000	1.0000	0.9999	0.9996	0.9987	0.9964	0.9915	0.9819	0.9648
7	1.0000	1.0000	1.0000	1.0000	1.0000	0.9999	0.9998	0.9993	0.9983	0.9961
$n = 9, x = 0$	0.6302	0.3874	0.2316	0.1342	0.0751	0.0404	0.0207	0.0101	0.0046	0.0020
1	0.9288	0.7748	0.5995	0.4362	0.3003	0.1960	0.1211	0.0705	0.0385	0.0195
2	0.9916	0.9470	0.8591	0.7382	0.6007	0.4628	0.3373	0.2318	0.1495	0.0898
3	0.9994	0.9917	0.9661	0.9144	0.8343	0.7297	0.6089	0.4826	0.3614	0.2539
4	1.0000	0.9991	0.9944	0.9804	0.9511	0.9012	0.8283	0.7334	0.6214	0.5000
5	1.0000	0.9999	0.9994	0.9969	0.9900	0.9747	0.9464	0.9006	0.8342	0.7461
6	1.0000	1.0000	1.0000	0.9997	0.9987	0.9957	0.9888	0.9750	0.9502	0.9102
7	1.0000	1.0000	1.0000	1.0000	0.9999	0.9996	0.9986	0.9962	0.9909	0.9805
8	1.0000	1.0000	1.0000	1.0000	1.0000	1.0000	0.9999	0.9997	0.9992	0.9980
$n = 10, x = 0$	0.5987	0.3487	0.1969	0.1074	0.0563	0.0282	0.0135	0.0060	0.0025	0.0010
1	0.9139	0.7361	0.5443	0.3758	0.2440	0.1493	0.0860	0.0464	0.0233	0.0107
2	0.9885	0.9298	0.8202	0.6778	0.5256	0.3828	0.2616	0.1673	0.0996	0.0547
3	0.9990	0.9872	0.9500	0.8791	0.7759	0.6496	0.5138	0.3823	0.2660	0.1719
4	0.9999	0.9984	0.9901	0.9672	0.9219	0.8497	0.7515	0.6331	0.5044	0.3770
5	1.0000	0.9999	0.9986	0.9936	0.9803	0.9527	0.9051	0.8338	0.7384	0.6230
6	1.0000	1.0000	0.9999	0.9991	0.9965	0.9894	0.9740	0.9452	0.8980	0.8281
7	1.0000	1.0000	1.0000	0.9999	0.9996	0.9984	0.9952	0.9877	0.9726	0.9453
8	1.0000	1.0000	1.0000	1.0000	1.0000	0.9999	0.9995	0.9983	0.9955	0.9893
9	1.0000	1.0000	1.0000	1.0000	1.0000	1.0000	1.0000	0.9999	0.9997	0.9990

$p =$	0.05	0.10	0.15	0.20	0.25	0.30	0.35	0.40	0.45	0.50
$n = 12, x = 0$	0.5404	0.2824	0.1422	0.0687	0.0317	0.0138	0.0057	0.0022	0.0008	0.0002
1	0.8816	0.6590	0.4435	0.2749	0.1584	0.0850	0.0424	0.0196	0.0083	0.0032
2	0.9804	0.8891	0.7358	0.5583	0.3907	0.2528	0.1513	0.0834	0.0421	0.0193
3	0.9978	0.9744	0.9078	0.7946	0.6488	0.4925	0.3467	0.2253	0.1345	0.0730
4	0.9998	0.9957	0.9761	0.9274	0.8424	0.7237	0.5833	0.4382	0.3044	0.1938
5	1.0000	0.9995	0.9954	0.9806	0.9456	0.8822	0.7873	0.6652	0.5269	0.3872
6	1.0000	0.9999	0.9993	0.9961	0.9857	0.9614	0.9154	0.8418	0.7393	0.6128
7	1.0000	1.0000	0.9999	0.9994	0.9972	0.9905	0.9745	0.9427	0.8883	0.8062
8	1.0000	1.0000	1.0000	0.9999	0.9996	0.9983	0.9944	0.9847	0.9644	0.9270
9	1.0000	1.0000	1.0000	1.0000	1.0000	0.9998	0.9992	0.9972	0.9921	0.9807
10	1.0000	1.0000	1.0000	1.0000	1.0000	1.0000	0.9999	0.9997	0.9989	0.9968
11	1.0000	1.0000	1.0000	1.0000	1.0000	1.0000	1.0000	1.0000	0.9999	0.9998
$n = 15, x = 0$	0.4633	0.2059	0.0874	0.0352	0.0134	0.0047	0.0016	0.0005	0.0001	0.0000
1	0.8290	0.5490	0.3186	0.1671	0.0802	0.0353	0.0142	0.0052	0.0017	0.0005
2	0.9638	0.8159	0.6042	0.3980	0.2361	0.1268	0.0617	0.0271	0.0107	0.0037
3	0.9945	0.9444	0.8227	0.6482	0.4613	0.2969	0.1727	0.0905	0.0424	0.0176
4	0.9994	0.9873	0.9383	0.8358	0.6865	0.5155	0.3519	0.2173	0.1204	0.0592
5	0.9999	0.9978	0.9832	0.9389	0.8516	0.7216	0.5643	0.4032	0.2608	0.1509
6	1.0000	0.9997	0.9964	0.9819	0.9434	0.8689	0.7548	0.6098	0.4522	0.3036
7	1.0000	1.0000	0.9994	0.9958	0.9827	0.9500	0.8868	0.7869	0.6535	0.5000
8	1.0000	1.0000	0.9999	0.9992	0.9958	0.9848	0.9578	0.9050	0.8182	0.6964
9	1.0000	1.0000	1.0000	0.9999	0.9992	0.9963	0.9876	0.9662	0.9231	0.8491
10	1.0000	1.0000	1.0000	1.0000	0.9999	0.9993	0.9972	0.9907	0.9745	0.9408
11	1.0000	1.0000	1.0000	1.0000	1.0000	0.9999	0.9995	0.9981	0.9937	0.9824
12	1.0000	1.0000	1.0000	1.0000	1.0000	1.0000	0.9999	0.9997	0.9989	0.9963
13	1.0000	1.0000	1.0000	1.0000	1.0000	1.0000	1.0000	1.0000	0.9999	0.9995
14	1.0000	1.0000	1.0000	1.0000	1.0000	1.0000	1.0000	1.0000	1.0000	1.0000
$n = 20, x = 0$	0.3585	0.1216	0.0388	0.0115	0.0032	0.0008	0.0002	0.0000	0.0000	0.0000
1	0.7358	0.3917	0.1756	0.0692	0.0243	0.0076	0.0021	0.0005	0.0001	0.0000
2	0.9245	0.6769	0.4049	0.2061	0.0913	0.0355	0.0121	0.0036	0.0009	0.0002
3	0.9841	0.8670	0.6477	0.4114	0.2252	0.1071	0.0444	0.0160	0.0049	0.0013
4	0.9974	0.9568	0.8298	0.6296	0.4148	0.2375	0.1182	0.0510	0.0189	0.0059
5	0.9997	0.9887	0.9327	0.8042	0.6172	0.4164	0.2454	0.1256	0.0553	0.0207
6	1.0000	0.9976	0.9781	0.9133	0.7858	0.6080	0.4166	0.2500	0.1299	0.0577
7	1.0000	0.9996	0.9941	0.9679	0.8982	0.7723	0.6010	0.4159	0.2520	0.1316
8	1.0000	0.9999	0.9987	0.9900	0.9591	0.8867	0.7624	0.5956	0.4143	0.2517
9	1.0000	1.0000	0.9998	0.9974	0.9861	0.9520	0.8782	0.7553	0.5914	0.4119
10	1.0000	1.0000	1.0000	0.9994	0.9961	0.9829	0.9468	0.8725	0.7507	0.5881
11	1.0000	1.0000	1.0000	0.9999	0.9991	0.9949	0.9804	0.9435	0.8692	0.7483
12	1.0000	1.0000	1.0000	1.0000	0.9998	0.9987	0.9940	0.9790	0.9420	0.8684
13	1.0000	1.0000	1.0000	1.0000	1.0000	0.9997	0.9985	0.9935	0.9786	0.9423
14	1.0000	1.0000	1.0000	1.0000	1.0000	1.0000	0.9997	0.9984	0.9936	0.9793
15	1.0000	1.0000	1.0000	1.0000	1.0000	1.0000	1.0000	0.9997	0.9985	0.9941
16	1.0000	1.0000	1.0000	1.0000	1.0000	1.0000	1.0000	1.0000	0.9997	0.9987
17	1.0000	1.0000	1.0000	1.0000	1.0000	1.0000	1.0000	1.0000	1.0000	0.9998
18	1.0000	1.0000	1.0000	1.0000	1.0000	1.0000	1.0000	1.0000	1.0000	1.0000

$p =$	0.05	0.10	0.15	0.20	0.25	0.30	0.35	0.40	0.45	0.50
$n = 25, x = 0$	0.2774	0.0718	0.0172	0.0038	0.0008	0.0001	0.0000	0.0000	0.0000	0.0000
1	0.6424	0.2712	0.0931	0.0274	0.0070	0.0016	0.0003	0.0001	0.0000	0.0000
2	0.8729	0.5371	0.2537	0.0982	0.0321	0.0090	0.0021	0.0004	0.0001	0.0000
3	0.9659	0.7636	0.4711	0.2340	0.0962	0.0332	0.0097	0.0024	0.0005	0.0001
4	0.9928	0.9020	0.6821	0.4207	0.2137	0.0905	0.0320	0.0095	0.0023	0.0005
5	0.9988	0.9666	0.8385	0.6167	0.3783	0.1935	0.0826	0.0294	0.0086	0.0020
6	0.9998	0.9905	0.9305	0.7800	0.5611	0.3407	0.1734	0.0736	0.0258	0.0073
7	1.0000	0.9977	0.9745	0.8909	0.7265	0.5118	0.3061	0.1536	0.0639	0.0216
8	1.0000	0.9995	0.9920	0.9532	0.8506	0.6769	0.4668	0.2735	0.1340	0.0539
9	1.0000	0.9999	0.9979	0.9827	0.9287	0.8106	0.6303	0.4246	0.2424	0.1148
10	1.0000	1.0000	0.9995	0.9944	0.9703	0.9022	0.7712	0.5858	0.3843	0.2122
11	1.0000	1.0000	0.9999	0.9985	0.9893	0.9558	0.8746	0.7323	0.5426	0.3450
12	1.0000	1.0000	1.0000	0.9996	0.9966	0.9825	0.9396	0.8462	0.6937	0.5000
13	1.0000	1.0000	1.0000	0.9999	0.9991	0.9940	0.9745	0.9222	0.8173	0.6550
14	1.0000	1.0000	1.0000	1.0000	0.9998	0.9982	0.9907	0.9656	0.9040	0.7878
15	1.0000	1.0000	1.0000	1.0000	1.0000	0.9995	0.9971	0.9868	0.9560	0.8852
16	1.0000	1.0000	1.0000	1.0000	1.0000	0.9999	0.9992	0.9957	0.9826	0.9461
17	1.0000	1.0000	1.0000	1.0000	1.0000	1.0000	0.9998	0.9988	0.9942	0.9784
18	1.0000	1.0000	1.0000	1.0000	1.0000	1.0000	1.0000	0.9997	0.9984	0.9927
19	1.0000	1.0000	1.0000	1.0000	1.0000	1.0000	1.0000	0.9999	0.9996	0.9980
20	1.0000	1.0000	1.0000	1.0000	1.0000	1.0000	1.0000	1.0000	0.9999	0.9995
21	1.0000	1.0000	1.0000	1.0000	1.0000	1.0000	1.0000	1.0000	1.0000	0.9999
22	1.0000	1.0000	1.0000	1.0000	1.0000	1.0000	1.0000	1.0000	1.0000	1.0000
$n = 30, x = 0$	0.2146	0.0424	0.0076	0.0012	0.0002	0.0000	0.0000	0.0000	0.0000	0.0000
1	0.5535	0.1837	0.0480	0.0105	0.0020	0.0003	0.0000	0.0000	0.0000	0.0000
2	0.8122	0.4114	0.1514	0.0442	0.0106	0.0021	0.0003	0.0000	0.0000	0.0000
3	0.9392	0.6474	0.3217	0.1227	0.0374	0.0093	0.0019	0.0003	0.0000	0.0000
4	0.9844	0.8245	0.5245	0.2552	0.0979	0.0302	0.0075	0.0015	0.0002	0.0000
5	0.9967	0.9268	0.7106	0.4275	0.2026	0.0766	0.0233	0.0057	0.0011	0.0002
6	0.9994	0.9742	0.8474	0.6070	0.3481	0.1595	0.0586	0.0172	0.0040	0.0007
7	0.9999	0.9922	0.9302	0.7608	0.5143	0.2814	0.1238	0.0435	0.0121	0.0026
8	1.0000	0.9980	0.9722	0.8713	0.6736	0.4315	0.2247	0.0940	0.0312	0.0081
9	1.0000	0.9995	0.9903	0.9389	0.8034	0.5888	0.3575	0.1763	0.0694	0.0214
10	1.0000	0.9999	0.9971	0.9744	0.8943	0.7304	0.5078	0.2915	0.1350	0.0494
11	1.0000	1.0000	0.9992	0.9905	0.9493	0.8407	0.6548	0.4311	0.2327	0.1002
12	1.0000	1.0000	0.9998	0.9969	0.9784	0.9155	0.7802	0.5785	0.3592	0.1808
13	1.0000	1.0000	1.0000	0.9991	0.9918	0.9599	0.8737	0.7145	0.5025	0.2923
14	1.0000	1.0000	1.0000	0.9998	0.9973	0.9831	0.9348	0.8246	0.6448	0.4278
15	1.0000	1.0000	1.0000	0.9999	0.9992	0.9936	0.9699	0.9029	0.7691	0.5722
16	1.0000	1.0000	1.0000	1.0000	0.9998	0.9979	0.9876	0.9519	0.8644	0.7077
17	1.0000	1.0000	1.0000	1.0000	0.9999	0.9994	0.9955	0.9788	0.9286	0.8192
18	1.0000	1.0000	1.0000	1.0000	1.0000	0.9998	0.9986	0.9917	0.9666	0.8998
19	1.0000	1.0000	1.0000	1.0000	1.0000	1.0000	0.9996	0.9971	0.9862	0.9506
20	1.0000	1.0000	1.0000	1.0000	1.0000	1.0000	0.9999	0.9991	0.9950	0.9786
21	1.0000	1.0000	1.0000	1.0000	1.0000	1.0000	1.0000	0.9998	0.9984	0.9919
22	1.0000	1.0000	1.0000	1.0000	1.0000	1.0000	1.0000	1.0000	0.9996	0.9974
23	1.0000	1.0000	1.0000	1.0000	1.0000	1.0000	1.0000	1.0000	0.9999	0.9993
24	1.0000	1.0000	1.0000	1.0000	1.0000	1.0000	1.0000	1.0000	1.0000	0.9998
25	1.0000	1.0000	1.0000	1.0000	1.0000	1.0000	1.0000	1.0000	1.0000	1.0000

$p =$	0.05	0.10	0.15	0.20	0.25	0.30	0.35	0.40	0.45	0.50
$n = 40, x = 0$	0.1285	0.0148	0.0015	0.0001	0.0000	0.0000	0.0000	0.0000	0.0000	0.0000
1	0.3991	0.0805	0.0121	0.0015	0.0001	0.0000	0.0000	0.0000	0.0000	0.0000
2	0.6767	0.2228	0.0486	0.0079	0.0010	0.0001	0.0000	0.0000	0.0000	0.0000
3	0.8619	0.4231	0.1302	0.0285	0.0047	0.0006	0.0001	0.0000	0.0000	0.0000
4	0.9520	0.6290	0.2633	0.0759	0.0160	0.0026	0.0003	0.0000	0.0000	0.0000
5	0.9861	0.7937	0.4325	0.1613	0.0433	0.0086	0.0013	0.0001	0.0000	0.0000
6	0.9966	0.9005	0.6067	0.2859	0.0962	0.0238	0.0044	0.0006	0.0001	0.0000
7	0.9993	0.9581	0.7559	0.4371	0.1820	0.0553	0.0124	0.0021	0.0002	0.0000
8	0.9999	0.9845	0.8646	0.5931	0.2998	0.1110	0.0303	0.0061	0.0009	0.0001
9	1.0000	0.9949	0.9328	0.7318	0.4395	0.1959	0.0644	0.0156	0.0027	0.0003
10	1.0000	0.9985	0.9701	0.8392	0.5839	0.3087	0.1215	0.0352	0.0074	0.0011
11	1.0000	0.9996	0.9880	0.9125	0.7151	0.4406	0.2053	0.0709	0.0179	0.0032
12	1.0000	0.9999	0.9957	0.9568	0.8209	0.5772	0.3143	0.1285	0.0386	0.0083
13	1.0000	1.0000	0.9986	0.9806	0.8968	0.7032	0.4408	0.2112	0.0751	0.0192
14	1.0000	1.0000	0.9996	0.9921	0.9456	0.8074	0.5721	0.3174	0.1326	0.0403
15	1.0000	1.0000	0.9999	0.9971	0.9738	0.8849	0.6946	0.4402	0.2142	0.0769
16	1.0000	1.0000	1.0000	0.9990	0.9884	0.9367	0.7978	0.5681	0.3185	0.1341
17	1.0000	1.0000	1.0000	0.9997	0.9953	0.9680	0.8761	0.6885	0.4391	0.2148
18	1.0000	1.0000	1.0000	0.9999	0.9983	0.9852	0.9301	0.7911	0.5651	0.3179
19	1.0000	1.0000	1.0000	1.0000	0.9994	0.9937	0.9637	0.8702	0.6844	0.4373
20	1.0000	1.0000	1.0000	1.0000	0.9998	0.9976	0.9827	0.9256	0.7870	0.5627
21	1.0000	1.0000	1.0000	1.0000	1.0000	0.9991	0.9925	0.9608	0.8669	0.6821
22	1.0000	1.0000	1.0000	1.0000	1.0000	0.9997	0.9970	0.9811	0.9233	0.7852
23	1.0000	1.0000	1.0000	1.0000	1.0000	0.9999	0.9989	0.9917	0.9595	0.8659
24	1.0000	1.0000	1.0000	1.0000	1.0000	1.0000	0.9996	0.9966	0.9804	0.9231
25	1.0000	1.0000	1.0000	1.0000	1.0000	1.0000	0.9999	0.9988	0.9914	0.9597
26	1.0000	1.0000	1.0000	1.0000	1.0000	1.0000	1.0000	0.9996	0.9966	0.9808
27	1.0000	1.0000	1.0000	1.0000	1.0000	1.0000	1.0000	0.9999	0.9988	0.9917
28	1.0000	1.0000	1.0000	1.0000	1.0000	1.0000	1.0000	1.0000	0.9996	0.9968
29	1.0000	1.0000	1.0000	1.0000	1.0000	1.0000	1.0000	1.0000	0.9999	0.9989
30	1.0000	1.0000	1.0000	1.0000	1.0000	1.0000	1.0000	1.0000	1.0000	0.9997
31	1.0000	1.0000	1.0000	1.0000	1.0000	1.0000	1.0000	1.0000	1.0000	0.9999
32	1.0000	1.0000	1.0000	1.0000	1.0000	1.0000	1.0000	1.0000	1.0000	1.0000

$p =$	0.05	0.10	0.15	0.20	0.25	0.30	0.35	0.40	0.45	0.50
$n = 50, x = 0$	0.0769	0.0052	0.0003	0.0000	0.0000	0.0000	0.0000	0.0000	0.0000	0.0000
1	0.2794	0.0338	0.0029	0.0002	0.0000	0.0000	0.0000	0.0000	0.0000	0.0000
2	0.5405	0.1117	0.0142	0.0013	0.0001	0.0000	0.0000	0.0000	0.0000	0.0000
3	0.7604	0.2503	0.0460	0.0057	0.0005	0.0000	0.0000	0.0000	0.0000	0.0000
4	0.8964	0.4312	0.1121	0.0185	0.0021	0.0002	0.0000	0.0000	0.0000	0.0000
5	0.9622	0.6161	0.2194	0.0480	0.0070	0.0007	0.0001	0.0000	0.0000	0.0000
6	0.9882	0.7702	0.3613	0.1034	0.0194	0.0025	0.0002	0.0000	0.0000	0.0000
7	0.9968	0.8779	0.5188	0.1904	0.0453	0.0073	0.0008	0.0001	0.0000	0.0000
8	0.9992	0.9421	0.6681	0.3073	0.0916	0.0183	0.0025	0.0002	0.0000	0.0000
9	0.9998	0.9755	0.7911	0.4437	0.1637	0.0402	0.0067	0.0008	0.0001	0.0000
10	1.0000	0.9906	0.8801	0.5836	0.2622	0.0789	0.0160	0.0022	0.0002	0.0000
11	1.0000	0.9968	0.9372	0.7107	0.3816	0.1390	0.0342	0.0057	0.0006	0.0000
12	1.0000	0.9990	0.9699	0.8139	0.5110	0.2229	0.0661	0.0133	0.0018	0.0002
13	1.0000	0.9997	0.9868	0.8894	0.6370	0.3279	0.1163	0.0280	0.0045	0.0005
14	1.0000	0.9999	0.9947	0.9393	0.7481	0.4468	0.1878	0.0540	0.0104	0.0013
15	1.0000	1.0000	0.9981	0.9692	0.8369	0.5692	0.2801	0.0955	0.0220	0.0033
16	1.0000	1.0000	0.9993	0.9856	0.9017	0.6839	0.3889	0.1561	0.0427	0.0077
17	1.0000	1.0000	0.9998	0.9937	0.9449	0.7822	0.5060	0.2369	0.0765	0.0164
18	1.0000	1.0000	0.9999	0.9975	0.9713	0.8594	0.6216	0.3356	0.1273	0.0325
19	1.0000	1.0000	1.0000	0.9991	0.9861	0.9152	0.7264	0.4465	0.1974	0.0595
20	1.0000	1.0000	1.0000	0.9997	0.9937	0.9522	0.8139	0.5610	0.2862	0.1013
21	1.0000	1.0000	1.0000	0.9999	0.9974	0.9749	0.8813	0.6701	0.3900	0.1611
22	1.0000	1.0000	1.0000	1.0000	0.9990	0.9877	0.9290	0.7660	0.5019	0.2399
23	1.0000	1.0000	1.0000	1.0000	0.9996	0.9944	0.9604	0.8438	0.6134	0.3359
24	1.0000	1.0000	1.0000	1.0000	0.9999	0.9976	0.9793	0.9022	0.7160	0.4439
25	1.0000	1.0000	1.0000	1.0000	1.0000	0.9991	0.9900	0.9427	0.8034	0.5561
26	1.0000	1.0000	1.0000	1.0000	1.0000	0.9997	0.9955	0.9686	0.8721	0.6641
27	1.0000	1.0000	1.0000	1.0000	1.0000	0.9999	0.9981	0.9840	0.9220	0.7601
28	1.0000	1.0000	1.0000	1.0000	1.0000	1.0000	0.9993	0.9924	0.9556	0.8389
29	1.0000	1.0000	1.0000	1.0000	1.0000	1.0000	0.9997	0.9966	0.9765	0.8987
30	1.0000	1.0000	1.0000	1.0000	1.0000	1.0000	0.9999	0.9986	0.9884	0.9405
31	1.0000	1.0000	1.0000	1.0000	1.0000	1.0000	1.0000	0.9995	0.9947	0.9675
32	1.0000	1.0000	1.0000	1.0000	1.0000	1.0000	1.0000	0.9998	0.9978	0.9836
33	1.0000	1.0000	1.0000	1.0000	1.0000	1.0000	1.0000	0.9999	0.9991	0.9923
34	1.0000	1.0000	1.0000	1.0000	1.0000	1.0000	1.0000	1.0000	0.9997	0.9967
35	1.0000	1.0000	1.0000	1.0000	1.0000	1.0000	1.0000	1.0000	0.9999	0.9987
36	1.0000	1.0000	1.0000	1.0000	1.0000	1.0000	1.0000	1.0000	1.0000	0.9995
37	1.0000	1.0000	1.0000	1.0000	1.0000	1.0000	1.0000	1.0000	1.0000	0.9998
38	1.0000	1.0000	1.0000	1.0000	1.0000	1.0000	1.0000	1.0000	1.0000	1.0000

Answers

CHAPTER 1

1.1 Populations and samples

1 a The whole set of items that are of interest.

   b A census observes or measures every member of a population.

   c A selection of observations taken from the population.

2 a An individual unit of a population.

   b A (numbered) list of the sampling units.

3 a Advantage: it should give a completely accurate result. Disadvantages: time consuming and expensive; cannot be used when the testing process destroys the item; hard to process large data sets.

   b Advantages: less time consuming and expensive; less data to process. Disadvantage: the data may not be representative of the population.

4 a Not sensible: too time consuming. Sensible: will use all of the data and give an accurate result.

   b Take a sample. Advantages: quicker and cheaper; less data to process afterwards.

5 a The loaves will be damaged by squashing them so there will be none left to sell.

   b A very small sample size, so may not be reflective of the overall proportion.

   c Taking a larger sample will improve the reliability.

6 a Time consuming/costly; hard to process all of the data.

   b The individual residents of the town.

   c The electoral register of voters does not include people who are ineligible to vote, such as those under the age of 18, and may also be incomplete since there may be residents who have not registered to vote.

7 a A census will destroy all the bulbs.

   b i While the average is greater than 800, one of the bulbs tested lasted less than 800 hours; so the claim is justified on average, but not on the basis that it refers to all of the bulbs.

      ii Increase the number of bulbs that are sampled.

1.2 Sampling

1 a A simple random sample of size n is one where every sample of size n has an equal chance of being selected.

   b Put the population into an ordered list (sampling frame) and generate 20 random numbers using the random number function on a calculator.

2 a The required items are chosen at regular intervals from an ordered list. The first item is chosen at random.

   b Choose the first item randomly (such as by using a random number generator) and then select every 5th item from the population.

3 a A sample which is proportional to the number of items in each strata/group.

   b Calculate the proportion of each group required in the sample (8 and 12) and then select these at random from an ordered list.

4 a Easy and cheap to carry out; each pupil has a known and equal chance of being selected.

   b The simple random sample may not reflect the proportions of boys and girls at the school.

   c The teacher should divide the sample size into the same proportion as the population and then randomly select the (15) boys and (25) girls.

5 a Generate the number of the first employee to be chosen randomly and then select every 20th employee from the ordered list of employee numbers.

   b The sampling frame is not random so the sampling method can introduce bias, for example if the first person chosen has a number ending in 0, all of the employees chosen will have a number ending in 0 and the entire sample will consist of managers.

6 a Number the students, perhaps by using their admission number, and then randomly generate 50 numbers. Disadvantages include the fact that the population is (fairly) large and that it might not be representative of the different age/year groups of pupils.

   b Stratified sampling; divide the sample into the same proportion as the proportion of students in each year (possibly split male/female too) and choose the required number of students randomly from each individual group.

1.3 Non-random sampling

1 a Opportunity sampling consists of taking the first n people who are available at the time of the research.

   b Stand in the street and ask the first 20 people who pass by and are prepared to answer questions.

2 a The sample is chosen so that it reflects the characteristics of the whole population.

   b Allocate quotas to each film showing at a large cinema. Select people who buy tickets for each film in order until the quota is fulfilled.

3 a Take the first 5 players from the ordered list.

   b These players will be the five shortest (or tallest) players and are unlikely to be representative of the team as a whole.

   c Take a simple random sample by generating five random numbers and selecting these players from the (numbered) ordered list.

4 a Opportunity sampling; the data is unlikely to be representative since the researchers ask a very small sample of people in a very specific location.

   b Take a larger sample of people; vary the time, day and location of the research.

5 a Divide the sample into the same proportion as the population to create each quota (30 males and 40 females), assign each person the researcher meets to a quota, then continue to ask/observe people until each quota is full.

   b In a stratified sample, the people selected in each group will be generated randomly; in a quota sample they will be the first n people the researcher meets.

c A stratified sample needs a sampling frame, which may not be available to the researcher.

d The researcher does not know that the driver owns the car that is being driven and does not know that the driver actually lives on the estate.

1.4 Types of data

1   **a**   Quantitative   **b**   Qualitative   **c**   Quantitative

2   **a**   Continuous   **b**   Discrete   **c**   Continuous

3   **a**   It is measured and can take any value.

     b   **i**   45 and 50   **ii**   5   **iii**   47.5

4   **a**   Discrete

     b   Divide the sample in the same proportion as the different strata (number of caterpillars) and choose from each stratum at random. Proportions are 8, 4, 6, 2.

     c   Continuous (quantitative) data

1.5 The large data set

1   **a**   Leuchars   **b**   Camborne   **c**   Camborne

2   **a**   Amount of precipitation including snow and hail that falls during a 24-hour period; measured in mm.

     b   Highest instantaneous windspeed recorded on a particular day; measured in knots.

3   **a**   **i**   It is too small.

         ii   It uses two locations that are almost the same latitude as each other.

     b   She can assign each date a number and then use a random number generator to generate the 15 dates in the sample.

     c   The sample should contain 15 different dates: data values cannot be reused. She should therefore reject the repeated value in the random number generation and generate a 16th random number.

4   **a**   Leuchars is further north.

     b   The sample size is very small; Jerome should increase the sample size to give a more representative sample.

5   **a**   Generate a random starting number then count on every 9 dates (since $\frac{184}{20} \approx 9$).

     b   The notation 'tr' means trace (less than 0.05 mm). Amara's method is not suitable as she has discarded valid data values.

     c   Any data value given as 'tr' should be recorded as 0 for the purpose of carrying out any calculations.

6   **a**   Daily maximum gust must be greater than or equal to the daily mean windspeed.

     b   4; Moderate

7   **a**   Hurn   **b**   Beijing   **c**   Perth

Problem solving: Set A

B   **a**   Generate five random numbers and select the dates from a numbered (ordered) list.

     b   Advantage: it is quick and easy to carry out. Disadvantage: it may not be representative of the whole data set.

     c   Take a larger sample.

S   **a**   Systematic sampling.

     b   There are only 92 days in these three months so her sample will be of size 18 or 19 (depending on the starting number).

G   **a**   Select five days at random from each month using a random number generator.

     b   The data is bound to be taken across all three months, ensuring proportional representation of each month.

     c   As a bearing; as a cardinal (compass) direction.

Problem solving: Set B

B   **a**   Opportunity sampling.

     b   Quick and easy to carry out.

     c   Increase the number of people he asks; vary the time of day he asks people.

S   **a**   Systematic sampling.

     b   Advantage: quick and easy to carry out. Disadvantage: not necessarily representative (limited time/location).

     c   Advantage: is likely to be representative of the students as a whole. Disadvantage: a sampling frame is required.

     d   Systematic sampling: a sampling frame is likely to be available – a register of students, for example.

G   **a**   It is in the middle of the day on a weekend, so more people are likely to be out shopping; the chosen location is central.

     b   For example, male shoppers under 40, female shoppers under 40, male shoppers 40 and over, female shoppers 40 and over.

     c   For example, use the electoral register to determine the size of each group as a proportion of the whole population, then assign the quotas as the same proportion of the whole sample.

CHAPTER 2

2.1 Measures of central tendency

1   **a**   450 g   **b**   444 g (3 s.f.)   **c**   450 g

2   **a**   4   **b**   3.69 (3 s.f.)   **c**   4

3   **a** $15 \leqslant t < 20$ **b**   18.6 minutes (3 s.f.)

4   1.65 m (3 s.f.)

5   **a**   6   **b**   5.78 (3 s.f.)

     c   It will increase it.

6   **a** $6 \leqslant t < 8$ **b**   6 minutes

     c   The midpoint has been used to estimate the time each customer in each class interval has spent in the store.

7   **a** $24 \leqslant t < 26$ **b**   23.5 °C (3 s.f.)

2.2 Other measures of location

1   **a**   313 g   **b**   372 g

2   **a**   3   **b**   4   **c**   2

3   **a**   4.25 km   **b**   6 km

4   **a**   16   **b**   14

5   **a**   50.4 kg (3 s.f.)

     b   It is assumed that the frequency in each class is evenly distributed throughout the interval.

6   **a**   **i**   32.9 cm (3 s.f.)   **ii**   36.3 cm (3 s.f.)

     b   The 90th percentile is in the last class which has no upper class boundary.

7 **a** 6.56 minutes (3 s.f.)

  b The data is evenly distributed within each class.

  c The 80th percentile is 8.83 mins (3 s.f.) so the advertisement is incorrect. In fact, 20% of trains are delayed by more than 8.83 minutes.

2.3 Measures of spread

1 **a** 15 cm **b** 5 cm

2 **a** 4 **b** 2

3 **a** 8 minutes **b** 2.37 minutes (3 s.f.)

4 **a** Median 5.15 knots; interquartile range 1.7 knots

  b The median daily mean windspeed was higher for the 10 days in May and there was less variability in windspeeds.

5 **a** 100 g

  b It will be less than this as it is unlikely that there is a value of 400 g and there cannot be a value of 500 g.

  c 31.9 g (3 s.f.) **d** 33 kittens

6 The 5% and 95% percentiles are 3.33 and 18.8 so the company is understating the wait times.

2.4 Variance and standard deviation

1 **a** 2.22 (3 s.f.) **b** 1.49 (3 s.f.)

2 **a** 293 **b** 1.18 (3 s.f.)

3 **a** 40.6 kg (3 s.f.) **b** 6.37 kg (3 s.f.)

4 **a** Mean 6.68 ladybirds; standard deviation 1.02 ladybirds

  b The mean number of ladybirds is higher on the second day, but there was less variability.

5 **a** Mean 5 hours; standard deviation 0.540 hours (3 s.f.)

  b One standard deviation from the mean gives [4.46, 5.54], which gives a frequency of 15 inside this interval. This is only 62.5% of the rounds, so Jez is wrong.

6 Mean 5.23 (3 s.f.); variance 6.83 (3 s.f.)

7 0.856 °C (3 s.f.)

2.5 Coding

1 **a** 6 7 8 4 5 8 7

  b 6.43 (3 s.f.) **c** 64.3 (3 s.f.)

2 **a** 8 **b** 3 **c** 9

3 **a** 220p or £2.20 **b** 89.4p

4 **a** 1009 hPa (4 s.f.) **b** 70.41 hPa^2

5 **a** Coding makes large numbers easier to manage.

  b $a = \frac{1}{5000}$ and $b = -20$

Problem solving: Set A

B 4

S 2.69 hours (3 s.f.)

G **a** 57.0 (3 s.f.) **b** 25%

  c That the scores are evenly distributed throughout the class, or that next year's scores will be similarly distributed to this year's scores.

Problem solving: Set B

B **a** Mean 5.70 hours (3 s.f.); standard deviation 2.05 hours (3 s.f.)

  b It is assumed all of the data points in each class are equal to the midpoint of the class interval.

S **a** 3.94 (3 s.f.) **b** 0.514 kg (3 s.f.)

  c It is assumed all of the data points in each class are equal to the midpoint of the class interval.

G **a** The last class is open-ended.

  b The manager could assume a maximum value for the class, such as 100.

  c Using 100 as the upper class boundary of the last class gives a mean of £26 590.

  d There could be a single very high value (such as the salary of the CEO) that makes the assumption in part **b** invalid.

CHAPTER 3

3.1 Outliers

1 **a** Yes **b** No **c** Yes

2 **a** No **b** Yes **c** No

3 **a** Yes; greater than 2 standard deviations from the mean.

  b 1.9 m; 1.1 m

  c No; it could be a legitimate data value, for example, a very mature adult snake.

4 **a** 0; 82

  b There are people that live to be 103 years old.

5 **a** 15.4; 2.58 (3 s.f.) **b** Yes; greater than 20.56.

  c 21 is too old to be a secondary school student.

  d 14.8; 1.87 (3 s.f.)

6 **a** 28.9 °C; 5.15 °C (3 s.f.)

  b Outliers are less than 18.6 and greater than 39.2, so 18.5 and 42.6 are outliers.

  c 18.5 no, it could just be a very cold day; 42.6 yes, it is an extreme value that does not fit the data.

  d Mean 27.6 °C, standard deviation 3.21 °C (3 s.f.)

3.2 Box plots

1

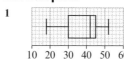

2 **a** 51 goals **b** 28 goals **c** 57 goals

3 **a** An outlier

  b Spread of masses is very similar but females, on average, weigh more than males.

  c Female: only one male bird has a mass greater than this, but between 25% and 50% of females have a mass greater than 3.6 g.

4 **a** Median = 7 knots, interquartile range = 4 knots

  b 16 and 19 are outliers.

  c

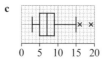

3.3 Cumulative frequency

1 a

Height (cm)	Cumulative frequency
$130 \leqslant h < 140$	15
$140 \leqslant h < 150$	33
$150 \leqslant h < 160$	56
$160 \leqslant h < 170$	70

b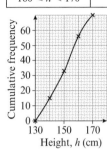

2 a 90 g   **b** 10.4 g

3 a 200   **b** 60.5 minutes   **c** 76 runners

4 a 61 days

   b Median 13.5 °C, interquartile range 4.1 °C

   c 19 days

   d She is assuming that the lowest recorded temperature is 8 °C and the highest recorded temperature is 20 °C but this might not be the case since the data is grouped. The lowest temperature could actually be 10 °C and the highest any value greater than 18 °C.

5 66% (approximately)

3.4 Histograms

1 a 0.5   **b** 7, 26, 38, 10, 4

2 a The classes are of unequal width.

   b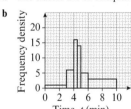

3 a Continuous data; classes are of different widths.

   b Width 0.5 cm, height 4 cm

4 a 8   **b** 37.9% (3 s.f.)

5 a $p = 30$, $q = 70$ **b** 4.2

6 182

3.5 Comparing data

1 The daily total sunshine in Hurn is on average lower but has greater variability.

2 a Year 8: mean 6.3 minutes (2 s.f.), standard deviation 1.2 minutes (2 s.f.)

     Year 10: mean 7.9 minutes, standard deviation 2.5 minutes (2 s.f.)

   b Year 10 has a higher average time and the times are more variable.

3 a Leuchars: slightly smaller interquartile range and smaller range if the two outliers are ignored.

   b Yes: less variability in the gustiness of the wind for Camborne.

4 Male otters are generally longer (median approximately 78 compared to 72) and females have a greater variability in length (interquartile range approximately 15 compared to 11).

5 a 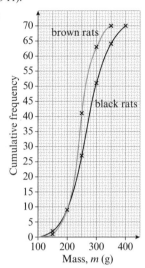   **b** Black rats

                 c Brown rats

Problem solving: Set A

B a Mean 4.2 seconds, standard deviation 2 seconds

     $4.2 + 2 \times 2 = 8.2$, and $8.3 > 8.2$, so is an outlier.

   b This is a reasonable amount of time taken to eat the biscuit, so it could be a legitimate data value.

S Mean 160.9 g, standard deviation 25.0 g (3 s.f.) Both values are outliers, but 223 g is a reasonable mass for a grapefruit, while 845 g is a much more extreme value so is likely to be an error. Only remove the 845 g value.

G Mean 39 ml, standard deviation 17.5 ml (3 s.f.)

     $Q_1 = 27$, $Q_3 = 51$, interquartile range 24

     Definition A produces one outlier (75).

     Definition B produces no outliers.

     Definition A is a more useful method of identifying extreme data values because it sets a lower and upper bound for acceptable data values. Definition B only sets an upper bound; $27 - 1.5 \times 24 = -9$, so even a value of 0 would not be regarded as an extreme value under this definition.

Problem solving: Set B

B 294 students

S 88 runners

G 71 or 72 swimmers

CHAPTER 4

4.1 Correlation

1 a Positive correlation   **b** No/zero correlation

   c Negative correlation

2 a

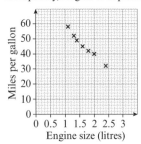

b Negative correlation

3 a Positive correlation

b As the daily mean temperature increases, the total daily sunshine increases.

c Accept July, August or September.

4 a

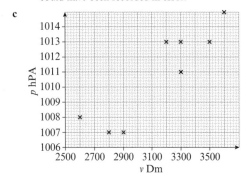

b Negative correlation. As the engine size increases, the car does fewer miles per gallon.

c Larger engines will need more fuel to run, so reasonable to assume a causal relationship.

5 a Positive correlation

b Unlikely to be causal as you don't know before the game how many goals will be scored. There could be a third variable that influences crowd size and number of goals scored, such as recent team performance.

6 a 2800 − 750 = 2050, so 1100 is an outlier.

b i Could have just been a particularly foggy day.
ii It is a long way away from the rest of the data so could have been recorded in error.

c

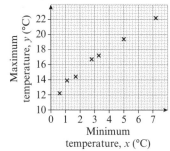

d Positive correlation.

e Yes. High pressure can cause less rain/cloud so could improve visibility.

4.2 Linear regression

1 a Graph A   **b** Graph C   **c** Graph B

2 a The initial mass of the coin is 3.56 g.

b The mass of the coin decreases by 0.012 g every hour.

3 a £290 000

b The increase in value (in £1000s) of an office block for each additional office.

c No. Buildings with no offices are likely to be retail outlets, or residential properties, and therefore will not fit the pattern of his data concerning office blocks.

4 a The mass, in grams, at birth; the increase in mass each day.

b This is outside the range of the data.

c This is the regression line for x on t. To predict age from mass, you would need the equation of the regression line for t on x.

5 a i Valid: inside the range of the data.

ii Invalid: outside the range of the data (extrapolating).

b This is the regression line for y on x. To predict temperature from pressure you would need the regression line for x on y.

c The data shows some degree of linear correlation, which suggests that the linear regression model will be a reasonable model for the data.

Problem solving

B a

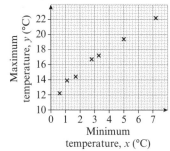

b The points appear to be close to a straight line.

c No: 12 is outside the range of the data, so this would be extrapolation.

S a The data exhibits a (very strong) linear trend.

b The value, in £1000s, when the flat is right in the centre of the city; the decrease in value for every 1 km from the city centre.

c Outside the range of the data, so this would be extrapolation.

d It is likely to be valid, as the value is not unrealistic. It could be that that flat is in a more expensive area than the others sampled, or it could have significantly bigger rooms.

G a The visibility decreases by 93.3 Dm for each 1% increase in humidity.

b i 90% is within the range of the data, so would be sensible.

ii The daily maximum relative humidity in the UK never falls below about 60%, so not valid.

c High humidity is associated with mist and fog, so it is likely that the relationship could be causal.

d This is the regression line for y on x. To predict the humidity from the visibility you would need the equation of the regression line for x on y.

CHAPTER 5

5.1 Calculating probabilities

1 a $\frac{2}{13}$ **b** $\frac{6}{13}$ **c** $\frac{10}{13}$

2 a $\frac{1}{24}$ **b** $\frac{3}{4}$ **c** $\frac{1}{3}$

3 a $\frac{64}{89}$ **b** $\frac{32}{89}$

c The heights are evenly distributed within each class.

4 a $\frac{13}{60}$ **b** $\frac{5}{12}$

c The masses are evenly distributed within each class.

5 a B4, B5, B6, B7, E4, E5, E6, E7, O4, O5, O6, O7

b i $\frac{1}{12}$ **ii** $\frac{1}{3}$

c 45, 46, 47, 54, 56, 57, 64, 65, 67, 74, 75, 76

d i $\frac{1}{6}$ **ii** $\frac{2}{3}$

5.2 Venn diagrams

1 a $\frac{11}{15}$ **b** $\frac{1}{3}$ **c** $\frac{14}{15}$

2

Tapioca   Semolina S

4 5 9

2

3 0.2

4 a 0.2 **b** 0.1

5 a 0.15 **b** 0.18

6 a $\frac{3}{7}$ **b** $\frac{9}{14}$

c $\frac{1}{10}$ **d** $\frac{9}{35}$

7 a $x = 0.18$, $y = 0.11$ **b** 0.32

8 a $3 + 6 = 9$; $\frac{9}{30} = \frac{3}{10}$ **b** $\frac{2}{3}$ **c** $\frac{1}{5}$

5.3 Mutually exclusive and independent events

1 a 0.75 **b** 0.25

2 a 0.2 **b** 0.3

3 0.24

4 0.17

5 a 0.05 **b** No: $0.5 \times 0.35 \neq 0.05$

6 $P(Y) = 0.4$; $P(Z) = 0.5$; $P(Y) \times P(Z) = 0.4 \times 0.5 \neq 0.25$

7 a C and D or C and E **b** $x = 0.15$; $y = 0.3$

c $P(D) \times P(E) = 0.35 \times 0.45 \neq 0.15$ therefore the student is not correct.

8 a F and I, since their circles do not overlap.

b $x = 0.25$; $y = 0.3$; $z = 0.05$

5.4 Tree diagrams

1 a

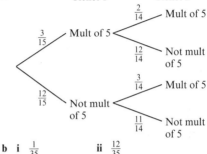

Counter 1   Counter 2

$\frac{4}{9}$ Red

$\frac{4}{9}$ Red $\quad \frac{4}{9}$ Red $\quad \frac{5}{9}$ Yellow

$\frac{5}{9}$ Yellow $\quad \frac{4}{9}$ Red $\quad \frac{5}{9}$ Yellow

b i $\frac{16}{81}$ **ii** $\frac{40}{81}$

2 a

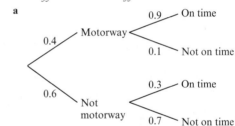

Ticket 1   Ticket 2

$\frac{3}{15}$ Mult of 5 $\quad \frac{2}{14}$ Mult of 5 $\quad \frac{12}{14}$ Not mult of 5

$\frac{12}{15}$ Not mult of 5 $\quad \frac{3}{14}$ Mult of 5 $\quad \frac{11}{14}$ Not mult of 5

b i $\frac{1}{35}$ **ii** $\frac{12}{35}$

3 a

0.4 Motorway $\quad$ 0.9 On time $\quad$ 0.1 Not on time

0.6 Not motorway $\quad$ 0.3 On time $\quad$ 0.7 Not on time

b No: P(on time) is different for each of the two initial choices.

c 0.46

4 a 0.216 **b** 0.288

c $\frac{343}{15625}$

5 a 5%

b P(B and not cured) $= 0.035 \neq$ P(B) $\times$ P(not cured) $(= 0.5 \times 0.06 = 0.03)$

6 a

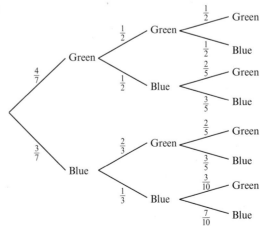

$\frac{4}{7}$ Green $\quad \frac{1}{2}$ Green $\quad \frac{1}{2}$ Green $\quad \frac{1}{2}$ Blue $\quad \frac{1}{2}$ Blue $\quad \frac{2}{5}$ Green $\quad \frac{3}{5}$ Blue

$\frac{3}{7}$ Blue $\quad \frac{2}{3}$ Green $\quad \frac{2}{5}$ Green $\quad \frac{3}{5}$ Blue $\quad \frac{1}{3}$ Blue $\quad \frac{3}{10}$ Green $\quad \frac{7}{10}$ Blue

b $\frac{3}{7}$

c $P(R) = \frac{4}{7} \times \frac{1}{2} \times \frac{1}{2} + \frac{4}{7} \times \frac{1}{2} \times \frac{3}{5} + \frac{3}{7} \times \frac{2}{3} \times \frac{3}{5} + \frac{3}{7} \times \frac{1}{3} \times \frac{7}{10}$

$= \frac{41}{70}$

d $\frac{17}{70}$

e No: $P(Q) \times P(R) \neq P(Q \text{ and } R)$

Problem solving: Set A

B **a** $x = 0.3, y = 0.1$

b $P(A) \times P(B) = 0.55 \times 0.4 \neq P(A \text{ and } B) (= 0.3)$

S **a** $(0.28 + x)(x - 0.24 + x) = x$ (because of independence)

$2x^2 + 0.32x - 0.0672 = x$

$2x^2 - 0.68x - 0.0672 = 0$

b $x = 0.42, y = 0.12$

c Other solution ($x = -0.08$) would give negative probabilities, so should be rejected.

G $x = 0.3, y = 0.2$

Problem solving: Set B

B **a**

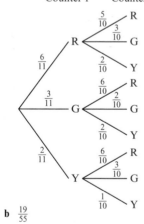

Token 1   Token 2

$\frac{6}{9}$ Orange

$\frac{6}{9}$ Orange

$\frac{3}{9}$ Green

$\frac{3}{9}$ Green

$\frac{6}{9}$ Orange

$\frac{3}{9}$ Green

b $\frac{4}{9}$

S **a**

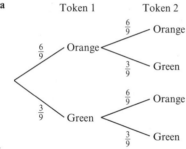

Counter 1   Counter 2

$\frac{6}{11}$ R

$\frac{5}{10}$ R

$\frac{3}{10}$ G

$\frac{2}{10}$ Y

$\frac{3}{11}$ G

$\frac{6}{10}$ R

$\frac{2}{10}$ G

$\frac{2}{10}$ Y

$\frac{2}{11}$ Y

$\frac{6}{10}$ R

$\frac{3}{10}$ G

$\frac{1}{10}$ Y

b $\frac{19}{55}$

G $\frac{2348}{6825}$

CHAPTER 6

Student answers may differ slightly from those shown here depending on whether tables or calculators were used.

6.1 Probability distributions

1 **a** Yes, 6 discrete outcomes, will occur randomly.

b No, time is a continuous variable.

c No, since it is fixed as always being 24.

2 **a**

x	1	2	3	4	5	6
$P(X = x)$	$\frac{1}{6}$	$\frac{1}{6}$	$\frac{1}{6}$	$\frac{1}{6}$	$\frac{1}{6}$	$\frac{1}{6}$

b $P(X = x) = \frac{1}{6}, x = 1, 2, 3, 4, 5, 6$

c The range of possible outcomes is a specific set of discrete variables where the probability of each occurring is the same.

3 **a** 6

b

y	1	2	3
$P(Y = y)$	$\frac{1}{6}$	$\frac{2}{6}$	$\frac{3}{6}$

c **i** $\frac{5}{6}$ **ii** 0

4 **a** 0.25   **b** 0.63   **c** 0.69

5 **a** $k + 2k + 3k + 4k + 5k = 1$ therefore $k = \frac{1}{15}$

b $\frac{4}{5}$

6 **a** $\frac{23}{120}$ **b** $\frac{31}{120}$

7 **a** Discrete uniform distribution

b **i** $\frac{1}{4}$ **ii** $\frac{4}{5}$ **c** $\frac{81}{400}$

8 **a**

x	1	2	3	4
$P(X = x)$	0.28	0.22	0.22	0.28

b 0.2016

9

x	1	2	3	4	5
$P(X = x)$	$\frac{4}{7}$	$\frac{12}{49}$	$\frac{36}{343}$	$\frac{108}{2401}$	$\frac{81}{2401}$

6.2 The binomial distribution

1 **a** Yes; fixed number of independent trials, two possible outcomes and fixed probability of success.

b No; not a fixed number of trials.

c No; not a fixed probability of success.

d Yes; fixed number of independent trials, two possible outcomes and fixed probability of success.

2 **a** 0.24576   **b** 0.01536   **c** 0.65536

3 **a** 0.1766   **b** 0.0639   **c** 0.2253

4 **a** $n = 8, p = 0.8$

b **i** 0.1468   **ii** 0.0092   **iii** 0.5033

5 **a** The lifetimes are independent of each other, there are a fixed number of trials, the probability that a battery lasts less than 30 hours is constant.

b 0.2242   **c** 0.5631

6 **a** $X \sim B(50, 0.8)$

b **i** 0.1398   **ii** 0.0013

7 **a** $X \sim B(10, 0.5)$

The rolls are independent of each other; the probability of rolling a prime number is constant.

b 0.2051   **c** 0.2803

6.3 Cumulative probabilities

1 **a** 0.2528   **b** 0.8822   **c** 0.0386

2 **a** 0.7869   **b** 0.0338   **c** 0.6046

3 **a** 0.8632   **b** 0.0138   **c** 0.9890

4   **a**   0.8034   **b**   0.0082   **c**   0.1938

5   **a**   0.0612   **b**   0.3429   **c**   0.1099

6   **a**   She has calculated the probability of greater than 4 sixes, not at least. She has not included the probability that $X = 4$.

     b   0.61846

7   **a** $X \sim B(40, 0.2)$ **b**   4   **c**   12   **d**   0.9283

8   **a**   **i**   0.1181   **ii**   0.0093

     b   She has worked out the probability of *greater than* 8 and not included the probability of 8 itself. Correct probability = 0.2131

Problem solving: Set A

B   **a**   10

     b

X	1	2	3	4
$P(X = x)$	$\frac{1}{10}$	$\frac{1}{5}$	$\frac{3}{10}$	$\frac{2}{5}$

     c $\frac{7}{10}$

S   **a**   0.23   **b**   0.34

G   **a**   The probability of a cat catching a mouse is constant; the attempts are independent.

     b   0.05792   **c**   0.128   **d**   0.05   **e**   0.2

     f   Karen's model assumes that the probability of catching the mouse is constant whereas Ian's model assumes that the probability increases with each attempt.

       OR, in Karen's model the cat may not catch the mouse, whereas in Ian's model the cat will definitely catch the mouse in its first five attempts.

Problem solving: Set B

B   **a** $Y \sim B(35, 0.64)$

     b   **i**   0.0043   **ii**   0.2491

S   **a**   2   **b**   9   **c**   0.9423

G   **a**   0.2332   **b**   0.0127

CHAPTER 7

7.1 Hypothesis testing

1   **a**   The number of threes Alice rolls.

     b $H_0: p = 0.25$ **c** $H_1: p > 0.25$

2   **a**   One   **b**   One   **c**   Two

3   **a**   The number of people in the sample who say they support the MP.

     b $H_0: p = 0.65$, $H_1: p < 0.65$

     c   If the probability of 24 or fewer people in the sample supporting the MP (with $p = 0.65$) is less than or equal to the significance level (5%).

4   **a**   The number of packets of cereal in the sample that contain a prize.

     b $H_0: p = 0.05$, $H_1: p > 0.05$

     c   If the probability of 15 or more packets containing a prize (with $p = 0.05$) is greater than the significance level (10%).

5   **a**   The number of cars in the sample that take less than or equal to 2 hours to complete the service.

     b $H_0: p = 0.6$, $H_1: p \neq 0.6$

     c   If the probability of 45 or more services taking less than two hours (with $p = 0.6$) is less than half the significance level.

7.2 Finding critical values

1   **a** $0 \leqslant X \leqslant 2$ **b**   4.98%

2   **a** $8 \leqslant X \leqslant 15$ **b**   5.00%

3   **a** $0 \leqslant X \leqslant 6$ and $16 \leqslant X \leqslant 25$ **b**   7.15%

4   **a**   The number of plants in the sample that have blue flowers. $H_0: p = 0.2$, $H_1: p < 0.2$

     b $0 \leqslant X \leqslant 2$ **c**   4.42%

5   **a**   The number of 5-star reviews in the sample. $H_0: p = 0.6$, $H_1: p > 0.6$

     b $16 \leqslant X \leqslant 20$ **c**   5.10%

6   **a** $X \sim B(n, 0.05)$; $H_0: p = 0.05$, $H_1: p \neq 0.05$

     b   0 and $5 \leqslant X \leqslant 50$ **c**   18.1%

7   **a** $\{0 \leqslant X \leqslant 3\}$ and $\{13 \leqslant X \leqslant 50\}$

     b   5.07%

7.3 One-tailed tests

1   Reject H_0 (prob = 0.016)

2   Accept H_0 (prob = 0.017)

3   **a** $X \sim B(n, 0.9)$

     b $H_0: p = 0.9$, $H_1: p < 0.9$. Accept H_0 (prob = 0.0995)

4   **a** $H_0: p = 0.6$, $H_1: p > 0.6$ **b**   23 or more

     c   25 is in the critical region so reject the null hypothesis; there is evidence to support the manufacturer's claim.

5 $H_0: p = 0.1$, $H_1: p < 0.1$; probability of one or no pots fracturing given $p = 0.1$ is 0.0338 which is less than 5%, so reject the null hypothesis; there is evidence that the new clay has reduced the likelihood of the pot fracturing.

6   Briony has calculated $P(X = 7)$ rather than $P(X \geqslant 7)$. $P(X \geqslant 7) = 0.0106 > 0.01$, so accept H_0.

7   **a**   0.5367

     b $H_0: p = 0.05$; $H_1: p > 0.05$
       Given $X \sim B(26, 0.05)$, $P(X \geqslant 4) = 0.0387 < 0.05$ so reject H_0: there is evidence the salesman has increased his likelihood of making a sale.

7.4 Two-tailed tests

1   Accept H_0 (prob = 0.0905)

2   Reject H_0 (prob = 0.0238)

3 $H_0: p = 0.05$, $H_1: p \neq 0.05$; accept H_0 since probability of 16 or more people having the disease is $0.0444 > 0.025$. The proportion of people who have the disease in the south west is not different from the national average.

4   **a** $X \leqslant 1$ and $X \geqslant 10$ **b**   5.83%

     c   2 is in the acceptance region, so no evidence to suggest the new diet has changed the proportion of clients who are overweight.

5 $H_0: p = 0.125$, $H_1: p \neq 0.125$; probability of 25 or more 8s given $p = 0.125$ is $0.0068 < 0.025$, so evidence that the dice is biased.

6   **a** $X \leqslant 3$ or $X \geqslant 12$ **b**   8.81%

     c   11 lies in the acceptance region so accept H_0.

Answers

7   H_0: $p = 0.02$; H_1: $p \neq 0.02$. $P(X \geqslant 3) = 0.0784 > 0.05$ so accept H_0. There is no evidence to suggest that the probability of getting a double yolk is different.

Problem solving: Set A

B   a $X \leqslant 5$ or $X \geqslant 17$ b   3.46%

   c   16 lies within the acceptance region so accept the null hypothesis.

S   a $X \leqslant 10$ or $X \geqslant 21$ b   0.08909

   c   22 lies within the critical region so reject the null hypothesis.

G   a $X \leqslant 3$ or $X \geqslant 13$ b   0.00184

Problem solving: Set B

B H_0: $p = 0.65$, H_1: $p \neq 0.65$. Probability of 13 or more given $p = 0.65$ is 0.0617 which is greater than 0.05 so no evidence to support the circus owner's belief.

S   a   0.4

   b H_0: $p = 0.4$, H_1: $p \neq 0.4$. Probability of 28 or more 4s given $p = 0.4$ is 0.0160 which is less than 0.025 so reject H_0: there is evidence to support Doreen's claim.

G   The employee has calculated the probability in the wrong tail: $P(X \geqslant 5)$ should be calculated. The employee has not halved the significance level in making a comparison with the probability. $P(X \geqslant 5 \mid p = 0.004) = 0.0076 < 0.025$ so reject H_0: there is evidence that the rate of defects has changed.

CHAPTER 8

8.1 Constructing a model

1   a   i   0 m   ii   1.26 m   iii   1.44 m

   b   −4.5 m

   c   Model is not valid when $x = 15$ as height would be 4.5 m below ground level.

2   a   8 m   b   6 m   c   −28 m

   d   The model is not valid when $t = 3$. After the diver enters the water, other forces then act on the diver and so the model ceases to be valid.

3   a   i   1.4 m   ii   2.75 m   iii   3 m

   b $h = -4$ m; so the model is not valid when $x = 20$ as the height would be below ground level.

4   a   142.4 m   b   The model is valid for $0 \leqslant t \leqslant 8$

5   $0 \leqslant x \leqslant 10$

6   $0 \leqslant t \leqslant 1.6$

7   a $0 \leqslant x \leqslant 16$ b   3.2 m

   c   Rashid throws the shot 16 m, Sam throws the shot 15 m. Rashid wins by 1 m.

8   a   1.8 m   b $x = 2$ and $x = 4$

   c $0 \leqslant x \leqslant 5$ d   3.6 m

8.2 Modelling assumptions

1   a   Ignores the rotational effect of any external forces that are acting on the see-saw, and the effects of air resistance.

   b   Ignores the width of the see-saw and assumes that the weight acts at the midpoint of the rod.

   c   This presumes the support is dimensionless and fixed, and ignores any frictional effects on the rod.

   d   Ignores the frictional effects on the children due to air resistance.

2   a   Ignores the friction between the racetrack and the car.

   b   The assumption is not valid; the racetrack will exert frictional forces on the car.

3   The bungee cord will stretch under the weight of the jumper.

4   Model the car and trailer as particles connected by a light rod.

   Ignore the effects of air resistance.

5   a   Model the stone as a particle, ignore the effects of air resistance.

   b   i   The motion will be identical.

      ii   The feather will take longer to fall.

   c   Include air resistance in the model, for example.

8.3 Quantities and units

1   a $12.5 \,\text{ms}^{-1}$ b $0.03 \,\text{kg} \,\text{s}^{-1}$ c $7000 \,\text{kg} \,\text{m}^{-3}$

   d $0.54 \,\text{kg} \,\text{m}^{-3}$ e $120 \,\text{kg} \,\text{m}^{-3}$ f $4.1 \times 10^8 \,\text{kg} \,\text{m}^{-3}$

2   a A: Air resistance, B: Weight.

   b A: Normal reaction, B: Friction or air resistance, C: Weight, D: Forward thrust.

   c A: Buoyancy, B: Tension, C: Weight, D: Water resistance or drag.

8.4 Working with vectors

1   a   42 mph   b   12 miles   c   −28 mph

   d   −9 miles   e   −34 mph

2   a   iii   b   ii   c   i   d   iv

3   a $14.4 \,\text{ms}^{-1}$ (3 s.f.)   b   56.3° (3 s.f.)

4   a $8.60 \,\text{ms}^{-2}$ (3 s.f.)   b   54.5° (3 s.f.)

5   a   27.2 km (3 s.f.)   b   17.1° (3 s.f.)

6   a   733.9 m (4 s.f.)   b   1216 m

   c   109.9° (4 s.f.)

Problem solving: Set A

B   a   i   2 m   ii   1.8 m   iii   0.8 m

   b $h = -3.6$ m, so the model is not valid when $x = 10$ as the model predicts the ball would be 3.6 m below the ground.

S   a   1.2 m   b $0 \leqslant x \leqslant 6$

   c $1 < k < 4$ d   2.45 m

G   32.7 m (3 s.f.)

Problem solving: Set B

B   a $7.81 \,\text{ms}^{-1}$ (3 s.f.)   b   50.2° (3 s.f.)

S   a   Yes.

     Distance travelled = 233.24 + 234.31 + 262.49 + 63.25
                          = 793.29 km < 800 km

   b   198°

G $a = 300$

CHAPTER 9

9.1 Displacement–time graphs

1 **a** A: 48 km h^{-1}, B: 0 km h^{-1}, C: -32 km h^{-1}

   b 0 km h^{-1} **c** 21.3 km h^{-1} (3 s.f.)

2 **a** 390 miles   **b** 52 mph   **c** 48.75 mph

3 **a** A: 25 km h^{-1}, B: 0 km h^{-1}, C: -30 km h^{-1},
      D: 0 km h^{-1}, E: 10 km h^{-1}

   b 5 hours 40 minutes   **c** 4 hours 15 minutes

   d 13.3 km h^{-1}

4 **a** 8 m   **b** 8.5 m, 0.3 s   **c** 0 m s^{-1}

   d **i** She travels upwards and her speed decreases.

       ii She travels downwards and her speed increases.

9.2 Velocity–time graphs

1 **a** 150 m   **b** 0.15 m s^{-2}

2 **a**

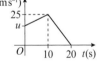

   b 2.25 m s^{-2}

   c 288 m

3 **a**   **b** 1.2 m s^{-2}

           c 540 m

           d 240 m

4 **a**

   b 25

5 **a**   **b** 15

6 **a**   **b** 12.5

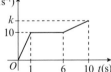

           c 0.625 m s^{-2}

   d Rate of acceleration decreases as velocity increases.

9.3 Constant acceleration formulae 1

1 53 m s^{-1} 2 0.45 m s^{-2} 3 28 m

4 40 seconds   5 21 m s^{-1} 6 11.5 m s^{-1}

7 **a** 2.5 seconds   **b** 22.5 m

8 **a** 14 m s^{-1} **b** 0.16 m s^{-2}

9 **a** 0.5 m s^{-2} **b** 225 m

   c 10 m s^{-1} **d** 100 m

10 **a** 40 seconds   **b** 0.25 m s^{-2}

11 Alex

---

12 **a** $57 = \dfrac{22 + v}{2} \times 3 \Rightarrow v = 16\,\text{m s}^{-1}$

      $16 = 22 + a(3) \Rightarrow a = -2\,\text{m s}^{-2}$

   b 121 m

13 **a** At $t = 5$, $15 = u + 5a$; at $t = 15$, $29 = u + 15a$.

      So $3u - u = (3 \times 15) - 29 \Rightarrow u = 8\,\text{m s}^{-1}$

      $a = 1.4\,\text{m s}^{-2}$

   b 57.5 : 220

9.4 Constant acceleration formulae 2

1 24.8 m s^{-1} (1 d.p.)   2 1.6 m s^{-2} 3 140 m

4 3 m s^{-2} 5 17 m s^{-1} 6 8 seconds

7 No, the car will not stop before the sign.

8 250 m

9 **a** 19.0 m s^{-1} (1 d.p.)

   b Assumption of uniform acceleration seems to be
      incorrect. The car is accelerating at a lower rate in the
      first 200 m than in the final 300 m.

10 **a** 0.45 m s^{-2} **b** 27 m s^{-1}

11 **a** 2.7 m s^{-1} (1 d.p.)   **b** 23.6 m s^{-1} (1 d.p.)

12 25 seconds   13 13.5 s (1 d.p.)

14 **a** 15 m s^{-1} **b** 25 seconds

9.5 Vertical motion under gravity

1 **a** 9.8 m s^{-1} **b** 4.9 m

   c 12.5 m s^{-1} (3 s.f.) **d** 1.28 seconds (3 s.f.)

2 **a** 43.6 m   **b** 31.6 m s^{-1}

3 **a** 13.1 m s^{-1} **b** 22.9 m s^{-1}

4 **a** 6.6 m s^{-1} **b** 7.35 seconds (3 s.f.)

5 **a** 6.17 m (3 s.f.)   **b** 1.12 seconds (3 s.f.)

6 **a** 14 m s^{-1} **b** 2.86 seconds (3 s.f.)

7 **a** 1.95 seconds (3 s.f.) **b** 12.1 m s^{-1} (3 s.f.)

   c New time will be greater than 1.95 seconds.

8 10.6   9 1.10 seconds (3 s.f.)

10 13.7

11 **a** 8.08 (3 s.f.)   **b** 2.47 seconds (3 s.f.)

12 2.5 seconds

Problem solving: Set A

B **a**   **b** 1.1 m s^{-2}

                c 19.8 m

                d 33.3 (3 s.f.)

S **a**   **b** 26.7 (3 s.f.)

G **a**
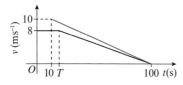
$T = 12.5$

b Deceleration of $P = 0.0914\,\text{m s}^{-2}$ (3 s.f.)
Deceleration of $Q = 0.111\,\text{m s}^{-2}$ (3 s.f.)
As rate of deceleration of Q is greater than the rate of deceleration of P the particles will only have the same instantaneous velocity if velocity of $Q = 8$ for some t where $10 < t < 12.5$.
Velocity of $Q = 10 + (-0.111)(t - 10)$
$10 + (-0.111)(t - 10) = 8 \Rightarrow t = 28 > 12.5$
The particles never have the same instantaneous velocity.

Problem solving: Set B

B **a** $19.1\,\text{m s}^{-1}$ **b** 13.275
S 2.82 seconds (3 s.f.)   **G** $25.7\,\text{m}$ (3 s.f.)

CHAPTER 10

10.1 Force diagrams

1 T **2** $12\,\text{N}$

   W

3 **a** $P = 15\,\text{N}$ **b** $P = 16\,\text{N}, Q = 24\,\text{N}$
   c $P = 20\,\text{N}, Q = 45\,\text{N}$

4 **a** $p = 8, q = 5$ **b** $p = 15, q = 10$
   c $p = 55, q = 70$

5 **a** **i** $\rightarrow 15\,\text{N}$ **ii** Particle will accelerate to the right
   b **i** $\downarrow 25\,\text{N}$ **ii** Particle will accelerate downwards

6 **a**
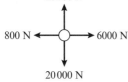
    b $5200\,\text{N}$ forwards

7 **a**
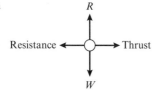
    b $3750\,\text{N}$

10.2 Forces as vectors

1 **a** $(i + j)\,\text{N}$ **b** $\binom{2}{1}\,\text{N}$
   c $(3i + 2j)\,\text{N}$ **d** $\binom{1}{4}\,\text{N}$
2 $a = -5, b = -1$
3 $a = 3, b = -1$

4 $a = 4, b = \frac{8}{3}$
5 **a** **i** $\sqrt{29}\,\text{N}$ **ii** $21.8°$ (1 d.p.)
   b **i** $5\,\text{N}$ **ii** $36.9°$ (1 d.p.)
   c **i** $\sqrt{41}\,\text{N}$ **ii** $141.3°$ (1 d.p.)
   d **i** $2\sqrt{10}\,\text{N}$ **ii** $161.6°$ (1 d.p.)
6 **a** **i** $(4i - 7j)\,\text{N}$ **ii** $\sqrt{65}\,\text{N}$ **iii** $150.3°$ (1 d.p.)
   b **i** $(3i - j)\,\text{N}$ **ii** $\sqrt{10}\,\text{N}$ **iii** $108.4°$ (1 d.p.)
7 **a** $a = 4, b = 3$ **b** $\sqrt{122}\,\text{N}$ **c** $5°$
8 **a** $a = 4, b = 2$ **b** $12\sqrt{2}\,\text{N}$ **c** $135°$
9 5

10.3 Forces and acceleration

1 $0.64\,\text{m s}^{-2}$ **2** $24\,\text{N}$ **3** $88.2\,\text{N}$
4 **a** $0.3\,\text{m s}^{-2}$ **b** 10 seconds
5 **a** $71.2\,\text{N}$ **b** $29.4\,\text{N}$ **c** $51\,\text{N}$
6 **a** $3.125\,\text{kg}$ **b** $1.72\,\text{kg}$ (3 s.f.)   **c** $2.85\,\text{kg}$ (3 s.f.)
7 **a** 5.2 **b** 7.93 (3 s.f.)   **c** 2.7
8 $20\,\text{N}$
9 **a** $588\,\text{N}$ **b** $618\,\text{N}$
10 **a** $1.2\,\text{m s}^{-2}$ **b** $9000\,\text{N}$
11 **a** 120 **b** $2.25\,\text{m}$

10.4 Motion in 2 dimensions

1 **a** $\left(\frac{3}{2}i + \frac{1}{4}j\right)\,\text{m s}^{-2}$
   b $\frac{\sqrt{37}}{4}\,\text{m s}^{-2}$ at $081°$ (to the nearest degree)
2 0.25
3 **a** $(50i - 30j)\,\text{N}$ **b** $10\sqrt{34}\,\text{N}$ at $121°$
4 **a** $(2i + 22j)\,\text{m s}^{-2}$ **b** $\left(\frac{11}{7}i - \frac{2}{7}j\right)\,\text{m s}^{-2}$
   c $\left(-\frac{5}{4}i - \frac{25}{12}j\right)\,\text{m s}^{-2}$ **d** $\left(\frac{6}{5}i - 4j\right)\,\text{m s}^{-2}$
5 **a** $1\,\text{m s}^{-2}$ at $-36.9°$ from i
   b 2 seconds   **c** $4.47\,\text{m s}^{-1}$ (2 s.f.)
6 $-2(p + 1) = q - 5 \Rightarrow -2p - 2 = q - 5 \Rightarrow 2p + q - 3 = 0$
7 $p = 8, q = -4$
8 **a** $9\sqrt{3}$ **b** $18\,\text{N}$
   c $6\,\text{m s}^{-2}$ **d** 5 seconds
9 **a** $p = 5, q = -12$ **b** $\frac{5\sqrt{50}}{13}\,\text{kg}$
10 4
11 **a** $63.4°$ (3 s.f.)
   b $2(q - 2) = (6 + p) \Rightarrow 2q - 4 = 6 + p \Rightarrow p - 2q + 10 = 0$
   c 2.5

10.5 Connected particles

1 **a** $6.4\,\text{N}$ **b** $4\,\text{N}$
2 **a** 12 **b** $20\,\text{N}$
3 **a** 2 **b** $30\,\text{N}$
4 **a** $21\,500\,\text{N}$
   b **i** $1290\,\text{N}$ upwards   **ii** $3440\,\text{N}$ downwards
5 **a** Lorry $3200\,\text{kg}$, trailer $8000\,\text{kg}$ **b** $44\,000\,\text{N}$
6 **a** 0.2 **b** $90\,\text{N}$
7 **a** $332\,\text{N}$ (3 s.f.)   **b** $148\,\text{N}$ (3 s.f.)

8 **a** 7200   **b** 44 100 N   **c** 7.41 m

    d Treating the tow-bar as inextensible is to assume that the acceleration of the lorry and the trailer are the same.

9 **a** $1.5\,\text{m s}^{-2}$ **b** 2850 N   **c** 709 N (3 s.f.)

10.6 Pulleys

1 **a** **i** $T - mg = ma$ **ii** $3mg - T = 3ma$

    b $0.5g\,\text{m s}^{-2}$

    c The magnitude of acceleration of the two particles is the same.

2 **a** $\frac{40}{13}g$ N   **b** 2.5

3 **a** **i** $\frac{3}{7}g\,\text{m s}^{-2}$ **ii** $\frac{20}{7}g$ N

    b $10.5\,\text{m s}^{-1}$ **c** 18.75 m

4 **a** 39 N   **b** 27   **c** 55.2 N (3 s.f.)

5 **a** $0.25g\,\text{m s}^{-2}$ **b** 0.756 s (3 s.f.)   **c** 1.68 m (3 s.f.)

Problem solving: Set A

B **a** $4000 - 400 - R = 2200 \times 1.5 \Rightarrow 3600 - R = 3300$
        $\Rightarrow R = 3600 - 3300 = 300$ N

    b 1800 N

S **a** 24 seconds

    b Unlikely, as resistance will decrease as speed decreases.

G **a** 500 N   **b** F will increase.

Problem solving: Set B

B **a** **i** $T - 2g = 2a$ **ii** $7g - T = 7a$

    b $a = \frac{5}{9}g\,\text{m s}^{-2}$

    c This means that you can assume that the tension in the string will be the same on both sides of the pulley.

S **a** $3.13\,\text{m s}^{-1}$ (3 s.f.) **b** 0.479 seconds (3 s.f.)

G 0.8 m

CHAPTER 11

11.1 Functions of time

1 **a** 16   **b** $\frac{2}{3}$ seconds

2 **a** $8\,\text{m s}^{-1}$ **b** $\frac{2}{3}$ seconds and 4 seconds

    c 5 seconds   **d** $\frac{25}{3}\,\text{m s}^{-1}$

3 **a** -2 m   **b** 5 m

4 **a** $\frac{25}{16}$ m   **b** 5 seconds

    c $\frac{25}{8}$ m   **d** $0 \leqslant t \leqslant 5$

5 $x = 3t(t - 2)^2 \geqslant 0$ for all $t \geqslant 0$.

6 **a** $t = 1.5$ and $t = 5$ seconds

    b $t = 0.5$ and $t = 6$ seconds   **c** $15\,\text{m s}^{-1}$

7 **a** 6 m

    b $5t^2 - t^3 = t^2(5 - t) \geqslant 0$ when $t \geqslant 0$ and $t \leqslant 5$, so $T = 5$

8 **a** $t = 0$ and $t = 10$ seconds   **b** $25\,\text{m s}^{-1}$

11.2 Using differentiation

1 **a** $47\,\text{m s}^{-1}$ **b** $6\,\text{m s}^{-1}$ **c** $0.75\,\text{m s}^{-1}$

2 **a** **i** $3t^3 + \frac{2}{t^3}$ **ii** $9t^2 - \frac{6}{t^4}$

    b **i** $18t^2 - 20t + 3$ **ii** $36t - 20$

    c **i** $\frac{3t^2}{2} - \frac{3}{4} - \frac{2}{t^2}$ **ii** $3t + \frac{4}{t^3}$

3 **a** $56\,\text{m s}^{-1}$ **b** $t = 0$ and $t = \frac{5}{3}$

    c $14\,\text{m s}^{-2}$

4 $-9\,\text{m s}^{-2}$

5 **a** 9 cm   **b** $6\,\text{cm s}^{-2}$

6 **a** $t = 1.5$ and $t = 7$ seconds

    b Greatest speed = $21\,\text{m s}^{-1}$ (when $a = 0$, $v = -15.125$)

7 **a** $k = 6$ **b** $10\,\text{m s}^{-2}$

8 **a**

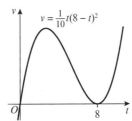

$v = \frac{1}{10}t(8 - t)^2$

    b $t = \frac{8}{3}$ s, $v = \frac{1024}{135}\,\text{m s}^{-1}$ and $t = 8$ s, $v = 0\,\text{m s}^{-1}$

11.3 Maxima and minima problems

1 **a** $s = 0$ at $t = 0$ and $t = 4$. s represents distance so must be positive. $s \geqslant 0$ when $0 \leqslant t \leqslant 4$.

    b 5.19 m

2 **a**

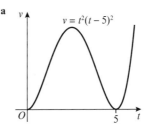

$v = t^2(t - 5)^2$

    b $v = 39.1$ m s^{-1} when $t = 2.5$ seconds

3 **a** 0.3 seconds   **b** 5.343 m   **c** -2.235 m s^{-1}

4 **a** 5 seconds

    b $s = t^3(5 - t)$

       For $0 \leqslant t \leqslant 5$, $t^3 \geqslant 0$ and $5 - t \geqslant 0$ so $s \geqslant 0$.

    c $s = 65.9$ m (3 s.f.)

5 5.832 m

6 **a** $b^2 - 4ac = 36 - 96 = -60 < 0$, so no real roots.

    b $5\,\text{m s}^{-1}$

7 Max distance is when

    $\frac{ds}{st} = 4.8 + 2.4t - 0.03t^2 = 0 \Rightarrow t = 82.0$ (3 s.f.).

    Max distance = 2.95 km (3 s.f.) so the train never reaches the end of the track.

8 $6\,\text{m s}^{-2}$

11.4 Using integration

1 **a** $v = \frac{4t^3}{3} - \frac{3t^4}{4}$ **b** $v = \frac{5t^2}{2} + \frac{t^3}{2}$ **c** $v = \frac{2t^3}{3} - \frac{t^2}{2}$

2 **a** **i** $s = \frac{t^4}{2} - \frac{t^2}{6} + t + c$ **ii** $s = 42$

    b **i** $s = \frac{t^4}{6} + \frac{t^5}{15} + c$ **ii** $s = 29.7$

    c **i** $s = \frac{5t^3}{3} + t^{\frac{3}{2}} + c$ **ii** $s = 50.2$ (3 s.f.)

Answers

3 $\frac{77}{3}$ m   **4** $\frac{16}{3}$ m

5 **a** $v = \frac{t^2}{2} - 3t + 4$ **b** $t = 2$ and $t = 4$ **c** $\frac{2}{3}$ m

6 $T = \frac{2}{5}$

7 Let $a = k(5 - t^2)$. Integrate this and use $v = 0$ when $t = 0$ and $v = 11$ when $t = 2$ to find k. Integrate again to find s and use $s = 0$ when $t = 0$.

8 38.6 m (3 s.f.)

11.5 Constant acceleration formulae

1 **a** $v = \dfrac{ds}{dt} = u + at$

    b Acceleration $= \dfrac{dv}{dt} = 0 + a = a$

2 **a** $v = \int a\,dt = at + c$. When $t = 0$, $v = u$, so $v = u + at$.

    b $s = \int v\,dt = ut + \frac{1}{2} at^2$

3 **b**: $a = 2$; **d**: $a = -1$; **e**: $v = 0$ (particle stationary)

4 **a** $AB = 850$ m

    b Acceleration $= \dfrac{d^2s}{dt^2} = \dfrac{d}{dt}(32 - 0.6t) = -0.6\ \text{m s}^{-2}$

5 **a** $v = \int 3\,dt = 3t + c$. $v = 10$ when $t = 0 \Rightarrow v = 3t + 10$

    b $s = \int (10 + 3t)\,dt = 10t + 1.5t^2 + c$

      $s = 5$ when $t = 0 \Rightarrow s = 10t + 1.5t^2 + 5$

6 $p = 3$, $q = -5$, $r = 6$

7 **a** $a = 4\ \text{m s}^{-2}$ **b** $s = 3 + 5t + 2t^2$

Problem solving: Set A

B **a** $\frac{1}{3}$ and 5 seconds   **b** 50.8 m   **c** $t \geqslant \frac{8}{3}$ s

S **a** 32 m   **b** 50 m

G **a** $t^2 \geqslant 0$, $t^2 - 6t + 10 = (t - 3)^2 + 1 > 0$

    b **i** The particle is not moving in the same direction for the whole of the motion, so the displacement at $t = 3$ is not the distance the particle moves in the first three seconds of its motion.

      ii 3.125 m

Problem solving: Set B

B **a** $t = 6$ seconds   **b** 54 m

S **a** 6.75 m s^{-1} **b** 13.5 m

G **a** 87.7 m   **b** 6.5 seconds

Exam question bank

Section A: Statistics

1 **a** Get a numbered (ordered) list of the pupils, choose the first one at random and then pick every fourth pupil.

    b Choose at random from the lists of boys and girls in proportion to the total of each gender (19 boys, 21 girls).

2 **a** $X \sim B\left(10, \frac{1}{8}\right)$

    b **i** 0.3758   **ii** 0.3611

3 **a** Opportunity sampling.

    b Simple random sampling. Advantage: quick and easy; disadvantage: might not fairly represent the whole month.

      Systematic sampling. Advantage: representative across the whole month; disadvantage: might not get a sample of size 5 since data could be missing.

    c Continuous, as it can take any value within the range.

4 **a** 30: the temperature of the reaction with zero catalyst; 2.1: the increase in temperature for each additional gram of catalyst.

    b 100 is significantly outside the range of data used to calculate the regression line equation.

    c This is the regression line for h on x. To estimate the amount of catalyst that generates a specific temperature she should use the regression line for x on h.

5 **a** $\frac{32}{95}$

    b That the same day cannot be chosen twice (non-replacement)

6 **a** The testing is likely to damage the tomatoes.

    b 11   **c** 12.4 g (3 s.f.)

    d The standard deviation of the second farmer's crop is lower so there is evidence to suggest greater consistency, but her sample size is also very small and therefore the results are likely to be unreliable.

7 **a** The testing is to destruction so all of the inner tubes would be damaged.

    b While the *average* number of kPa is greater than 600, two-fifths of the sampled inner tubes burst below this pressure.

    c Sample more inner tubes.

8 **a** The value goes down as age goes up so the gradient of the regression line should be negative.

    b Evidence will probably be a scatter diagram, but the data does not follow a linear trend so a linear regression model is not suitable.

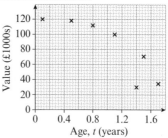

    c It could be due to very high mileage, or there could be some damage on the vehicle.

9 **a** An 'eighth', so oktas represent the number of eighths of the sky that is cloud-covered.

    b Discrete uniform distribution   **c** 0.25

    d It does not include the possibility that X could equal 0.

10 **a** A and C or B and C **b** 0.175

    c $P(A) \times P(B) = 0.475 \times 0.35 \neq P(A \text{ and } B)$ (which is 0.175)

11 **a** B and E **b** Outliers   **c** 4

12 **a** An okta is an eighth (of the sky covered by cloud), and takes integer values from 0 to 8. It is a discrete variable.

    b The points appear to form a curve, rather than a line.

    c Her data set is very small and taken from a single location in a single month.

13 **a** The person doing the survey asks the first n people they meet at a specific time and/or place.

    b Continuous. Time can take any value in the range. Just because it is rounded to the nearest hour does not negate this fact.

    c 8.53 hours (3 s.f.)

14 **a** $X \sim \text{B}(25, 0.25)$ **b** 0.0713   **c** 11

15 **a** Have an ordered list of dates, and generate 30 random numbers between 1 and 194.

b 7.54 kn (3 s.f.)

c Mean 7.73 kn (3 s.f); standard deviation 1.82 kn (3 s.f.)

16 **a** $k = \frac{6}{11}$ **b** $\frac{36}{121}$

x	1	2	3
$P(X = x)$	$\frac{6}{11}$	$\frac{6}{22}$	$\frac{6}{33}$

17 **a** An individual unit of a population.

b A numbered/ordered list of the sampling units in a given population.

c Generate 20 random numbers and then use those numbers to read off the data for the corresponding dates in the (ordered) list of dates.

d Free of bias; easy/cheap/quick to carry out; each sampling unit has a known and equal chance of being chosen.

18 **a** $X \sim \text{B}(24, 0.1)$

Each egg must be independent; the probability of an egg being cracked must be constant.

b 0.7075   **c** 0.1392

19 **a** Opportunity sampling

b Positive correlation

c The points lie in an approximate straight line.

d The additional bpm after exercise for each bpm for the resting heart rate.

e It is outside the range of the data (extrapolation).

20 **a** 5

b Median 7.56 kn, interquartile range 3.96 kn (3 s.f.)

c Hurn has lower daily mean windspeeds on average and a greater variability in daily mean windspeeds.

21 **a** $20 + 3 = 23$, so 31 is an outlier.

b It was recorded in error, or the data was misread.

c 13.2: the daily maximum gust when the daily mean windspeed is zero; 0.864: the increase in daily maximum gust for each knot the daily mean windspeed increases.

d Yes: days with higher mean windspeeds will tend to have higher maximum gusts.

22 **a** Median 46 g, interquartile range 5 g

b 11   **c** 68.68

23 **a** A fixed probability, p, of success (0.2) and two possible outcomes (illegal and legal).

b 0.1227   **c** $H_0: p = 0.2$, $H_1: p < 0.2$

d P(3 or fewer) $= 0.1227 > 0.10$, so there is insufficient evidence to support the Department of Transport's claim.

24 **a** Mean 2.1; variance 0.0525

b Mean 1018.4 hPa; standard deviation 0.917 hPa (3 s.f.)

c Increase the size of her sample.

25 **a** 7%

b $P(X) \times P(\text{spoilt}) = 0.2 \times 0.05 \neq P(X \text{ and spoilt})$ (which is 0.006)

26 **a** 110 runners

b Mean 3.03 hours, standard deviation 0.290 hours (3 s.f.)

27 **a** A region of a probability distribution which, if the test statistic falls within it, would cause you to reject the null hypothesis.

b $X \leqslant 3$ and $X \geqslant 13$ **c** 5.07%

d Savannah should accept it since 4 lies in the acceptance region. There is evidence that she is late to school with probability 0.3

28 **a** There are two outcomes: yellow and not yellow; the probability of success is assumed to be constant and the trials independent since there are a 'large number' of disks and there are a fixed number of trials.

b 0.3930   **c** 0.4771

29 **a** $X \leqslant 2$ or $X \geqslant 9$ **b** 10.7% (3 s.f.)

c Smaller: Donna has a 1.14% chance of incorrectly rejecting the null hypothesis.

30 **a** 6.43 (3 s.f.)   **b** 5.00 (3 s.f.)

c Median 22.86 minutes; standard deviation 10 minutes (using rounded values from **a** and **b**)

d No. The percentage of students in the sample finishing the puzzle in less than 16 minutes is 20.8%. So assuming the same distribution of times in the selection round, she will only get 9 students ($45 \times 20.8 = 9.36$).

31 **a** 0.1633   **b** 0.0468

c $H_0: p = 0.2$, $H_1: p > 0.2$

d Critical region is 9 or more (with a significance level of 5%) and since 9 lies in the critical region there is evidence to support Charlie's claim.

32 **a** 12.2; 4.12 (3 s.f.)   **b** $\frac{13}{30}$

c That the data is evenly distributed within each class.

33 **a** $\frac{11}{60}$

b 60; a in lowest terms has a denominator of 60 so since this is discrete data and there cannot be 'part students', 60 is the minimum number of students.

c **i** $\frac{9}{400}$ **ii** $\frac{11}{60}$

34 **a** Choose 7 days at random from each of the 6 months in the data set.

b The hypothesis that you assume to be correct.

c $H_0: p = 0.36$, $H_1: p > 0.36$

d Probability of 22 or more given $p = 0.36$ is 0.0218, which is less than 5% so there is evidence to support Maedeh's belief.

35 **a** She chose randomly from the students in each year group in proportion to the number of students in that year group.

b 8   **c** 0.84

d $0.4 \times 0.6 = 0.24 \neq 0.16$ so not independent.

36 **a** Opportunity sampling

b Quota sampling. She could ask the first people who fulfil certain characteristics, such as gender and age, until she has reached her quota for each type.

c Census   **d** 4.5 km

e Mean 7.7 km; standard deviation 3.32 km (3 s.f.)

Answers

f Median and interquartile range; since the data is skewed the mean and standard deviation are affected by the extreme values.

g Lower quartile and median will both increase since data values have moved from below the lower quartile to above the median.

Section B: Mechanics

37 a $1.13\,\mathrm{m\,s^{-2}}$ (3 s.f.)   **b** $8\,\mathrm{m\,s^{-1}}$

38 a 1.7 (2 s.f.)   **b** 22 N

39 a

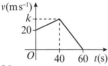

b 24

40 a 96 m   **b** $4 < t < 28$

41 $-4(p - 1) = 3(q + 3) \Rightarrow -4p + 4 = 3q + 9 \Rightarrow 4p + 3q + 5 = 0$

42 a i 720 m   **ii** $12\,\mathrm{m\,s^{-1}}$ **b** 23.6 seconds

43 a i 70 seconds   **ii** 820 m

b

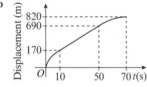

44 a $1.5\,\mathrm{m\,s^{-2}}$ **b** 4100 N

c Unlikely, as resistance to motion will increase as velocity increases.

45 a 8.1 m   **b** New value is lower

46 2.4375 m

47 a $a = 5, b = 2$ **b** $\sqrt{113}$ N   **c** 49°   **d** 59.8 m

48 a 10 m   **b** $16.3\,\mathrm{m\,s^{-1}}$ (3 s.f.)

c 3.09 seconds (3 s.f.)

49 a $\frac{5}{4}\,\mathrm{m\,s^{-2}}$ **b** $\frac{55}{12}\,\mathrm{m}$

50 a 480 m   **b** 275.5 m (4 s.f.)

51 a 4 and 8 seconds   **b** 12

52 a i 2.5   **ii** 2.86 seconds (3 s.f.)

b $12.1\,\mathrm{m\,s^{-1}}$ (3 s.f.)

c x will be smaller, because the speed after rebound will be lower.

53 a i $T - 2 = 0.5a$ **ii** $g - T = a$

b i 4.6 N   **ii** $5.2\,\mathrm{m\,s^{-2}}$

c 0.92 N

d The tension in the string is the same on both sides of the pulley.

54 a $s = t^4 - 8t^3 + 24t^2 - 32t + 16$

$v = \dfrac{\mathrm{d}s}{\mathrm{d}t} = 4t^3 - 24t^2 + 48t - 32$

$= 4(t^3 - 6t^2 + 12t - 8)$

$= 4(t - 2)^3 \geq 0$ for $t \geq 2$

So $k = 2$

b $a = \dfrac{\mathrm{d}v}{\mathrm{d}t} = 12t^2 - 48t + 48$

$= 12(t - 2)^2$

55 a i 9.29 s (3 s.f.)   **ii** $13.2\,\mathrm{m\,s^{-1}}$ (3 s.f.)

b For example, it is impossible for the acceleration of the sprinter to change instantaneously, so the graph could not have 'sharp corners'

56 a $v = 3t + \dfrac{1}{t^2} - 4$ **b** $s = \dfrac{3t^2}{2} - \dfrac{1}{t} - 4t + \dfrac{7}{2}$

57 a $\frac{8}{5}g$ N   **b** 1   **c** 2.75 m (3 s.f.)

58 $v = 6 - \dfrac{4}{t^2}$

59 a 16.6 N   **b** $1.98\,\mathrm{m\,s^{-1}}$

c Tension is equal throughout the system.   **d** 0.250 s (3 s.f.)

60 a $k = 56.4$ **b** 171.6 N

c Each particle (and the whole system) have the same acceleration.

d Speed of system after 2 seconds is $28.8\,\mathrm{m\,s^{-1}}$.
For A: $-56.4 = 8a \Rightarrow a = -7.05\,\mathrm{m\,s^{-2}}$
For B: $-56.4 = 5a \Rightarrow a = -11.28\,\mathrm{m\,s^{-2}}$
Using $v^2 = u^2 + 2as$, A would stop in 58.8 m (3 s.f.) and B would stop in 36.8 m (3 s.f.).
Since $36.8 + 20 < 58.8$, the particles will collide.